SPIRITUAL
GRANDPARENTING

SPIRITUAL
GRANDPARENTING

Bringing Our Grandchildren to God

THERESE M. BOUCHER

CROSSROAD • NEW YORK

1991

The Crossroad Publishing Company
370 Lexington Avenue, New York, NY 10017

Copyright © 1991 by Therese M. Boucher

All rights reserved. No part of this book may be reproduced, stored in a retrieval system, or transmitted, in any form or by any means, electronic, mechanical, photocopying, recording, or otherwise, without the written permission of The Crossroad Publishing Company.

Printed in the United States cf America
Typesetting output: TEXSource, Houston

Library of Congress Cataloging-in-Publication Data

Boucher, Therese.
    Spiritual grandparenting : bringing our grandchildren to God / Therese M. Boucher.
      p. cm.
    Includes bibliographical references.
    ISBN 0-8245-1060-7
    1. Family—Religious life. 2. Grandparenting. I. Title.
BX2351.B64   1991
248.8′4—dc20
                                             90-47895
                                               CIP

To
Walter and Jeannia Young
Lillian Howard
and
Edward Dolan

Contents

Introduction

*T*HE TINY FINGER SANDWICHES and cookies were sprinkled with tears. Our friends at St. Patrick's had assembled in the lower church hall to say good-bye. John and I were leaving Hudson after four years of ministry. The evening ended with Scripture, prayer, and music. Dick asked if he could say a blessing. We said yes. He thanked God for us and lifted all of our feelings and good-byes into God's presence.

Then our friend did a strange thing. He put his hands on our shoulders and prayed aloud for our grandchildren and great-grandchildren, asking God's protection and an awareness of God's incredible love. "Grandchildren?" I was surprised and disoriented. We were only thirty-seven! Our four children were handful enough. The business at hand was moving to a new state, not off into the distant future. But his blessing intrigued me, and still does.

I am connected to grandchildren I have never met, to grown people in another century. Curly-haired or blue-eyed, solemn or rambunctious, born or unborn, it doesn't matter. Something about me calls them into existence. What will that be? I have made a decision. I want that something to be God's love, empowering me to be a spiritual grandparent. Even now I can lift my children into the waiting arms of Jesus. I can pray for spouses they will choose and for grandchildren. I want my life to be an instrument for their eternal and outrageous happiness in his sight. I want to love them with God's love.

A grandchild is born with a delicious mixture of genes, talents, and even physical weaknesses from four grandparents and two parents. I believe that God has orchestrated that recipe. When we touch and hold and bless these little ones, God creates. I believe that God is at work in our hearts and families. There is a sharing of life across generations and across thousands of miles if necessary. We can be companions in the richest sense of the word, no matter what style of grandparenting we choose, no matter what our personality.

Spiritual Grandparenting considers the paths to intimacy that are at the center of grandparenting. God touches grandparents and children. Chapter 1 is an invitation to treasure the vision of wholeness that Jesus offers our families. Chapter 2 offers a way to deepen the meaning of holidays and visits. Chapter 3 discusses the need to balance a genuine affection for grandchildren with a respectful love for their parents. Chapter 4 develops story and history-sharing skills. Chapter 5 points out natural paths to God that are already a part of human life. Chapter 6 explores life-giving activities that build and celebrate relationships with our grandchildren. Chapter 7 invites a participation in God's love for grandchildren and their families who are experiencing crisis. The names of many individuals have been changed to protect their personal stories. After each chapter there are questions for personal reflection or small group discussion. There are also suggested activities that you might share with a grandchild.

This may seem like too many promises for one small book. What if your health is failing? What if grandchildren live three thousand miles away? What if these little ones have turned into distant, rebellious teens? What if your own children don't want to see you? What if they all move in with you? What then? I don't know, but I know someone who does. No promise or need is too overwhelming for Jesus, the Christ, Emmanuel, God-with-us.

Once a year our family makes a pilgrimage to Worcester, Massachusetts. We take the time to renew family relationships and explore the city where most of us were born. One place intrigues me. Behind city hall and the common with its reflecting pool is a mall and an office complex several stories high. This is ordinary enough. But within a few feet of this sprawling tribute to progress is Notre Dame, a hundred-year-old stone church with twin spires and sculpted archways. The architectural combination is jarring.

How would you respond to a church of cathedral proportions jammed next to a large office building and mall? Would you be saddened that the old landmark has no breathing space? What would the picture say to you? The key to what it says to me is in the central archway of the church. There sits a carving of Jesus on a heavenly throne. My parents were married inside. My mother did a colored pencil drawing of the old altar, a drawing that still hangs over our bed. I think the juxtaposition of church and mall say that God is real, just as real as shopping, work, and banking. If we have a relationship with Jesus, our religious heritage can be central to life.

It is in wrestling with such paradoxes that we will find hope for the future. Our lives and past have relevance alongside our grandchildren's lives. As we sort through what we want to share with our grandchildren, it is important to let Jesus sit over the doorways of our hearts. In acknowledging our love for God we can speak volumes to our grandchildren, even if we never say a word. We are spiritual grandparents. It is what we want most to give, a life that lasts forever, a happiness that is never outdated or out of place.

CHAPTER 1

Jesus Calls My Family to Wholeness

---

*I*T'S HARD TO DESCRIBE what Grandma and Grandpa can be to a small child, to a confused teenager, or to a grown person many years after their last meeting. There are so many intangibles involved. Each of us is different in how we experience love from the generations before and after us. A boy named Timothy gives us one picture:

> I like my grandparents! My grandpa made space suits for astronauts. My grandparents live in Boston. My grandma lives near the water. My grandpa likes to make spaghetti. I'm going to visit them on spring vacation. We will drive there. They're very nice to me.

I once met a woman I'll call Angela at a Bible study: Angela had another picture of grandparenting. When she was a child her parents did not practice any religion. She took that as normal. Then one day when she was about six, her grandmother invited her to ride to Mass with her on a parish bus. Five years of Sundays stretched on, providing time for a friendship that was unafraid of any subject or need. The old Italian woman even showed Angela a box under her bed with the clothes she wanted for burial. She gave her a treasured prayer book that Angela still uses thirty years later; but the more striking legacy was a life-long desire to learn about God. She is the only practicing Christian in her family, but that doesn't stop her from pursuing a deeper faith.

I know another woman named Emma from a broken past and childhood she would rather not discuss. Yet this experience has not left her with painful bitterness. Instead, she is convinced of the importance of reaching out to her own grandchildren. Emma enjoys showing them a backyard full of wild birds, or an occasional trip to the circus. She even saved money for a few years to bring them to Disneyland. Emma says with her own brand of explosive chuckling, "I'm the grandmother that I never had!"

Being a grandparent, or a grandchild, can put us on the brink of a "holy timelessness." A grandparent can look backward, rekindling experiences that have touched soul and heart, providing a window on the meaning of life for young ones. Both can look forward relishing unlived and reworked dreams held in common. The relationship can be like a ride in an open-air carriage with a view toward past, present, and future.

One grandmother likes to make this kind of sharing very concrete by playing "wagon train" with her little ones, just as she did with her own children. She puts a blanket over the kitchen table, or the sofa, and climbs underneath with a few pillows and a treasured toy. Grandparent and child pretend they are in a covered wagon and spin stories about what happens next. One story leads to another. Real life adventures and issues are rehearsed. As children get older she settles for wrapping up in a large blanket together. Older still, and she invites teenagers for a ride alone in her "wagon train" car. The mention of the old game opens the door for story swapping or problem solving, if the emotional weather permits.

Perhaps you have experienced this intimacy as a grandparent, or a grandchild. Maybe you haven't, but wanted to. As we explore grandparenting together, there are many friends and believers who are companions in the adventure of renewal and rebirth that spans the generations. The very nature of our experiences, good and bad, can also confirm the call that is deeply embedded in the human heart, the desire to be a spiritual grandparent.

Spiritual Grandparent

But why do some enjoy a lasting impression of being loved by older family members and others feel deprived? What gives some of us the knack for mixing day-to-day reality with living faith, so that it can be offered and appreciated by our grandchildren? And most important, what does this have to do with you and your family? "What makes a spiritual grandparent?" you might ask.

The ingredients are very common household items seen and experienced through the not-so-common vision of faith in Jesus, the Christ. That's all. That's ALL! First there is the birth of a child, but not just any unnamed infant from a Pampers' commercial. This child has been claimed and hallowed. We may not have experienced labor pains or financial nightmares, first hand; but we prize each tiny finger and wrinkle. We treasure and respect this new little person.

Next, comes the rebirth of a grandparent, who is plunged into a grappling and unique mid-life newness/oldness. Is my turn all over? Can I relish my own child's adulthood without feeling regrets or disappointment? Who does this little one say that I am?

Finally, there is the new relationship between grandparent and child, bonded one to the other, in the presence of God, who is Emmanuel. This is where we find the leaven that can heal, teach, and love as a quiet sign of God's Reign. Whether you or your children or grandchildren have ever graced the insides of a church, this is possible. Whether you live next door to them or three thousand miles away, this is already true. Even if you first claim a grandchild at age ten, through remarriage or a kind of "parish adoption," God can do this. As you acknowledge the birth and rebirth that is a part of grandparenting, healing and joy will be given and received. It happens in a hundred different ways.

There are many styles of grandparenting based in our different personalities and past experiences with life. Also, grandmothers are different from grandfathers. Finally, society's view of adult, parent, and child also shapes our expectations and goals. The world we live in offers patterns for human life, shepherding little children into play, then school. Adults are expected to work and raise families, then retire and "rest." These patterns can offer help or hindrance as we develop a style of grandparenting. It is important to choose only what will help us share the fullness of God's life, and discard the rest.

Donna was in the habit of letting her two grandsons stay for a long weekend once a year, while their parents enjoyed a "honeymoon" break. But this year was different. Donna's own mother had moved into her house and needed quite a bit of physical assistance on a day-to-day basis. She was torn by conflicting desires and needs, but decided that the extra work was manageable with a few adjustments in her routine. "It's quite an experience to have a three-year-old and a ninety-year-old at the same table!" she confided, "But it's worth it."

Choosing Patterns

There is a wisdom in Donna's decision to let people of all ages flourish together. This is not the opposite of a respect for the various needs of different age groups. We sense this. An earlier society sent ten-year-olds off to work in sweat shops and mills. The distinction between child and adult was blurred. Now children ease into responsibilities and family relationships. Yet today we struggle with another problem of stereotyping what each age group should do. Children are often entertained and indulged to the point of self-centered boredom. Meaningful service and accountability become foreign to such children.

Older adults are "freed" from the pressures of a work-oriented life at some point in time, yet can be troubled by a similar isolation from other generations in their families and parishes. New activities or relationships were promised as ways to express talents and personal interests, but the price of escaping is high. Some are shocked at how unimportant so many of the possibilities seem when not measured by dollars and cents. The challenge of deciding life's direction anew and being self-motivated can be hard to face.

Perhaps the restrictions of these stereotypes for children and retirees challenge us. We have passed through childhood and experienced life as working adults. We might also be experimenting with retirement and its expectations. Yet we know that no one of these stages has left us outrageously happy for years on end. A grandparent can play prophet by holding on to a vision of life that treasures work, play, rest, and education at every age. This can be a part of the timelessness of being a spiritual grandparent. The undercurrent of God's life can flood our souls in a new way, bringing a balance.

The quality of relationships with our grandchildren is also based in patterns of relating to our grown children. The ways we invested ourselves in them as they were launched from the nest provide a foundation. If all went well, the normal tug-of-war for independence brought us to the brink of a new friendship with these fledgling adults. We are free to love their children also. If not, there is work and God's grace ahead of us.

Sheila's Catholic son married a Jewish girl. Loving her new daughter-in-law stretched her to a new affection for people with different religious convictions. "After all, Jesus, my best friend, was a Jew!" she explained. Then came the day she learned that Debbie was pregnant. Sheila was elated, even excited about a child that would grow up without prejudice. She couldn't wait to see and hold the baby. The work she had done in letting go of her son freed her to enjoy her granddaughter.

Grandparenting: Gift of Companionship

What we enjoy most about being a grandparent tells us a lot about what God can do in the relationship. Let me ask you a most important question. When I say grandchild, who or what comes to mind? How do you feel? What do you see? How would you describe what has happened to you? What pains do you face in your family that need God's touch? Let me share a word-picture to nudge your imagination.

Once upon a time, there was a small but pleasant home on the edge of a quiet road that ended in Green Hill Park. Every gray front step had well-worn troughs in its center. There was a red wooden toy box in one corner of the porch and an old rocker on the other side in front of the living room window with the blue curtains. There were hash marks on the white door jamb; "Julie–48 inches" and "Mark–1962." Other scratched-over, but not forgotten, symbols decorated the railings. Grandma and Grandpa lived there....

This little portrait shows us one kind of grandparent. A most important gift is hospitality, which provides space for growing children, as well as neighbors, perhaps. If you can picture an open-ended love, no matter how the physical image looks, you have been blessed. You stand at the crux of the good news of God's very personal love. If not, Jesus is waiting to help and heal you.

I asked thirty people what they liked most about being grandparents. One woman answered, "Receiving true love from the young and innocent." A majority of grandparents liked watching children, appreciating their freedom, imagination, liveliness, and personalities. They were aware of growth and celebrated life through their grandchildren's activities.

Jesus has come into our fallen-down, crumpled universe with the forgiving, freeing love of the resurrection. That love is not someone else's fiction, but an intergenerational reality. Jesus has a personal relationship with each member of our families. He offers each one joy amid pain, life despite death. He is not limited by age or background. No mistakes in family life can obliterate his ever-present concern. It is accurate to imagine him sitting with us on the porch, or in the living room or the car, when we gather as family.

His love unleashes strength and vitality in grandparenting. We are not enslaved by family approval, physical illness, or broken relationships. God loves us. We can trust God for our changing needs. God gives us guidelines for midlife, redirecting our energies, our marriages. God gives us new courage to face a noisy little person with dirty diapers, or a disgruntled teen. We can forget ourselves once more in God. That urge to see, hold, and cherish is a gift we can enjoy by the power of God's Spirit within.

> Becoming a grandparent is a deeply meaningful event in a person's life. Seeing the birth of a grandchild can give a person a great sense of the completion of being, or immortality through the chain of generations.[1]

The New American Grandparent by Andrew J. Cherlin and Frank Furstenberg, Jr., describes a study done with 510 grandparents. About 30 percent experienced remote relationships with grandchildren. They saw themselves as formal figureheads from a previous era. The children experienced what I call the "my how you have grown" syndrome. External remarks hardly ever gave way to real personal conversation or activities together.

What gave the other 70 percent a chance to go beyond this pattern was spending time together in some regular way. These people experienced companionship with their grandchildren in varying degrees. Some enjoyed informal family gatherings and leisure activities together. A few, about 16 percent of all surveyed, had very involved relationships that included some parent-like behavior. The authors also note that it is common for one person to have all three kinds of relationships with different grandchildren; remote, companioned, and involved.

This book makes an important point. It would seem that the foundation of other grandparenting skills is the gift of ourselves to our young people. We love first by being present. The word "companion" comes from the Latin, meaning someone we eat bread with, sharing life in a primary way. This may not always translate into living just down the block, or even babysitting four hours every week. For most of us this is just not true or possible. What it does mean is some kind of individual care and attention, given in a reliable and regular fashion. Our technology is there to help us foster close relationships if we begin with imagination and commitment.

My mother-in-law gave herself to the task. When she married Dad, he was a widower with five children, who was more than twenty years her senior. This eventually made for a strange conglomeration of grandchildren, but they were all hers. Mum sent greeting cards to all of us. The cards always named the occasion and the relationship, "To a dear daughter-in-law" or "grandson." When Mum died last year twenty-eight of her thirty grandchildren came to the funeral. Each one had felt claimed and loved even though twenty were only "adopted" grandchildren.

Emotional Cement

Another study by Arthur Kornhaber and Kenneth L. Woodward helps us learn more about this kind of companionship. In *Grandparents/Grandchildren: The Vital Connection* they report a study done with three hundred children (through drawings) and three hundred grandparents (through interviews). The writers insist that emotional attachments are the cement of our human connectedness.

They found that 80 percent of the children studied had only sporadic contact with grandparents, 5 percent had close contact, and 15 percent had none at all. Children with sporadic contact expected some closeness at some point in their lives and often experienced rejection, disinterest, or confusion when it didn't happen. Children close to their grandparents in some way often experienced them as many things: nurturer, teacher, role model, wisdom figure, person of faith, historian, and oracle. We will explore these possibilities in later chapters.

No matter what category your own grandchildren fall into, there is hope for closer relationships. Our imperfect emotional attachments can be transformed by the merciful attention of God's Spirit. It is common to struggle with ways to be faithful as grandparents. This study can give us compassion for the mixed feelings a young person may experience, as we try to reach out. We should not be discouraged, but confident in God's love and attentive to underlying needs for family contact.

Peter is a teenager who would fall into the 80 percent with only a sporadic relationship with his grandfather. They saw each other about three times a year for day-long visits. The pair walked on the beach together, sometimes alone, sometimes not. Once as they walked, Pepere shared his boyhood family problems. Then he turned to Peter and said, "You're lucky. You have good parents and a good home. I wish I was you." In that regular act of walking together, and in that one little bit of intimate conversation, Peter experienced a word that touched his soul and endures in his memory.

Each of us can make a valuable contribution to our grandchildren's lives through this gift of companionship. People of different ages need each other. The child rekindles in us a sense of play, adventure, and surprise. The grandparent can add a sense of appreciation, a stepping back, a reflection on life that deepens the child. Timelessness can be shared.

Indicators for Faith-Sharing

When we become companions for our grandchildren the relationships we develop will touch many deeply human issues. As the prophet Joel says, "Old men will dream dreams and young men will see visions" (Joel 3:1). I remember coming home from an overnight stay at my grandmother's and describing her housekeeping tactics. "She puts the breakfast dishes on the table before she goes to bed and keeps a bowl of spoons on the table too!" I explained with excitement. My mother was not impressed. To my surprise she was actually disgruntled at my suggestion that we imitate her own mother. I was crushed. As a child I didn't realize how impractical such a plan would be to the mother of six. Today I realize that Memere's organized approach was much closer to my own inclinations. I don't set the table at night, but I do administrate religious education programs that require detailed planning. I also have a son with an organized mind. When he was less than three he wanted a detailed itinerary of our shopping trips. "Which store will we go to first, second, and last?" he wanted to know. Just like Memere with the spoons, I suspect.

Our ability to listen and reflect provides a springboard for exploring the values our grandchildren will choose for themselves as they grow up. We can affirm what is good and expand on what is lacking. Jack's two grandsons were telling him that they might have to move. Their dad was looking at other jobs. "Maybe we could live in a big house and be rich," they explained. Jack listened then remarked, "I know a lot of rich people!" Brian turned in surprise; but Luke smiled knowingly and said, "You mean people that love each other."

Jack's comment was more than a quip or a joke. It could be understood as faith-sharing. His vision of life and its ultimate meaning was very clear to the boys; yet he didn't lecture or preach. This is what is meant by witnessing on a level that young people can appreciate. Also, the lives we live speak. Choices we have made carry a message. Even though our love may be imperfect God's Reign can shine through.

Betty is an alcoholic like her mother before her. Betty's son is also an active alcoholic. Her grandson Eddie has suffered much, but he sees Betty reach out for help to Alcoholics Anonymous and to her parish prayer group. She is truthful about her needs. Betty hopes that her own humility and example will speak to Eddie and help him too.

Betty is typical of many Christians with a vision of wholeness for their families. They are grounded in a happiness that comes through God's personal intervention in daily life. It is as if they had received a magnifying glass trained on the immeasurable goodness that is possible for their children and grandchildren. This vision awakens a desire for the same experience in others. God's love is Trinity, expanding and flowing from person to person by its very nature.

Vision of Wholeness

This desire is a precious gift from God, a key element in the life of the spiritual grandparent. Perhaps you have experienced this. If you have, you also know its pain and cost. Problems and needs can also look larger when we want more for our loved ones. Even though we are sure that God loves family members, they don't always see Jesus with the same eyes.

Mary held her first grandson in the palm of one hand. The tiny premature infant was struggling just to breathe. She offered the little baby to God, and as she prayed, she knew the child would live and had a special role to play in God's plan. Her vision will be an important one as he grows up. But how will she communicate her experience that day in the newborn nursery?

In such situations it becomes crucial to rely on the witness of our lives and to share faith in simple ways. For now, Mary teaches this little preschooler songs about Jesus and his friends. His favorite describes Zaccheus in a tree. A Christian grandparent might also describe religious experiences through "I feel," not "you should" statements. For example, when looking at a sunset, statements like, "We should pray to the Creator now!" or "Be grateful for the beauty God has given," cannot be relied on to encourage faith. "I feel peaceful and close to God," might be better. Another comment might be "There is something about these colors that reminds me of God's beauty." Be careful of demands and expectations underneath our comments.

Grandchildren are also aware of our weaknesses. We must ask forgiveness when necessary, and expect God to heal them. I experienced such a healing as a young adult. As I recall, my grandmother did not approve of our apartment in the inner-city. "Why don't you buy a nice house?" she often asked when we would visit. I felt rejected. But God's love was at work too. As my husband and I established a routine of daily prayer together, I grew. Children, spouse, and relatives could be experienced with a new peace and security. I noticed small changes in myself and in important relationships.

During a visit to Memere the following year, she repeated her wish that we buy a house in the suburbs. I smiled and patted her wrinkled hand. I heard her say that she wanted a good life for us. I didn't fall into the old trap of sour indignation, imagining that she didn't like our apartment in the city. We had the same vision of happiness, just different ideas about how to achieve it. I realized too that she needed to see our place so she wouldn't worry. We arranged a visit and even carried her up a flight of stairs in a chair for a birthday party.

Kindred Spirits Find Each Other

God's nurturing presence in our relationships accomplishes more than we can ask or imagine. Our physical and genetic oneness can be more deeply forged as we become companions in faith. We can be shaped by our common baptism, Eucharist, and by the Word of God that we allow to enliven us. According to Uncle Eddie, we can become "kindred spirits."

Uncle Eddie was my Grandpa Fenner's brother. I didn't know either of them very well, or feel close to Grandpa Fenner as a child for a number of reasons. I remember meeting Uncle Eddie only once, at a picnic, when he was visiting from Ohio. We both enjoyed talking at length about all kinds of things. We noticed that we had many gifts and traits in common; then our conversation deepened. We began to share about Jesus. He was a common friend. When Uncle Eddie said good-bye he kissed my foot. It sounds silly but it was a very moving experience. I felt I had been claimed by the Fenners.

Each of us is a different person, yet somehow connected to those before and after us. Maybe it's the shape of a nose, or a penchant for jigsaw puzzles, or a whispering kind of a laugh. Our uniqueness washes up on the shores of a grandchild's personality and is mirrored back to us. There is a delicious ebb and flow of oneness. Life touches life. Kindred spirits meet when we see each other with God's eyes.

One of the tasks of a spiritual grandparent is looking with God's eyes for a child's gifts. Appreciation comes easily for many of us, but how deeply do we look into a little one's eyes as that child grows? The challenge is to let bonding happen and then continue between us, in whatever ways time, circumstance, and God's providence allow. As time goes on, the relationship will change and we will discover the child's special talents and personality in new ways.

The gifts we see may challenge us. An extroverted grandchild might need someone to be a hostess for his or her friends. A child who likes science might help us rediscover stargazing. This is why each grandchild has a different intimacy with us. Each one shows us a different part of ourselves. Perhaps some will lead us into experiences with our undeveloped side.

The urge to nurture and foster giftedness is so strong for some people that they have adopted grandchildren in their parishes or neighborhoods. The experience of being kindred spirits happens without genetic ties. One woman who owns a small store near us has no children of her own. But scores of young college people come "home" to visit her and tell her about their new lives. Carl and Stephanie have adopted a young troubled mother and her children into their extended family. The amount of healing this young woman has experienced, just being at family gatherings, is remarkable.

Pearl and Henry actually have a plan for parish "adoption" that they teach their friends. They sit near a family for a few weeks, greeting the parents and complimenting them on their children. Then they learn the children's names. One week they bring cookies and ask if they can give them to the children after Mass. The cookies are enjoyed outside together once a month. The visiting is weekly, even though it's only a few minutes. All kinds of variations develop.

Whether we are involved with our genetic or adopted grandchildren, the desire to love can be magnified by God. God will lead us to a genuine interest in our grandchild's daily life, his friends, her dreams. An overwhelming majority of grandparents that I surveyed, when asked what they liked to talk to a grandchild about, replied, "Whatever they are interested in. I just listen first." What a gift this is for these young people. What a blessing it is for their elders to experience themselves as grandparents of older children, not just babies. What an opportunity to build family life and teach ways of relating in love that will endure.

> Every time a child is born, a grandparent is born too.... A grandparent is reborn with each new grandchild.... Something happens.... For grandparents it is a gift of a new connection between all who have preceded them and all who proceed from them.[2]

We can see such things happen as gift from a Creator at work in our lives and hearts. We can be spiritual grandparents in our visiting, in our conversations, holiday celebrations, and crises. We can be spiritual grandparents when we say yes to the personal renewal and holy timelessness that God is offering us. We can reexamine our goals as grandparents, welcoming the kind of companionship and attachments that will help build the families of the next generations. Dreams and visions are meant to be a part of human life, an important part of grandparenting. Dreams and visions will become the foundation for sharing our faith in Jesus, the one who points the way to eternal life for all of us.

➤ ○ ➤

For Reflection, Sharing, and Discussion

1. What do you like about being a grandparent?

2. What do you find difficult about being a grandparent?

3. What grandparent did you feel closest to as a child? What did you like about this person? How are you the same or different? What did he or she teach you about grandparenting?

4. How has your faith in God helped you love your children and grandchildren? How have you been able to share that faith with them?

5. List your grandchildren. Next to each of their names write one or two things you like about that one.

6. Try a "getting to know you" quiz with a school-aged grandchild. Kids love to give adults tests. Ask them to write the answers to these questions on a paper *without showing you*. Then tell them what you think they wrote and find out your score. Perhaps the child would also like to take the test about you. (Don't stress the score if he or she does). Use what you both learn as a discussion starter.

"Getting to Know You" Quiz

1. My favorite ice cream is . . .

2. My favorite movie is . . .

3. My favorite color is . . .

4. My favorite place to be alone is . . .

5. My best friend is . . .

6. My worst nightmare was . . .

7. My least favorite thing is . . .

CHAPTER 2

Off to Grandma's for the Holidays

I ASKED PENNY how far it was to her grandmother's house.
She explained it this way:

> It's down the road, just two MacDonalds, then one sleep and
> muffins in the hotel room. Then you go across the turnpike,
> not the freeway. Go to the Burger King with the golden hats.
> After that, look for a fire station and a blue house. Then you
> take your suitcase out of the car and papers from under the
> seat and give kisses.

The whole experience of coming together for a holiday has
many important elements. There is often a lot of preparation and work, perhaps some travel. The journey can be as
complicated as the emotional and psychological re-entry after a crisis, or as simple as a child's return to the "feeling
place" that is Grandma's. Penny mentions one of our hopes
as we come together . . . the kisses. Holidays can be a time
to renew our relationships, to regroup and draw strength
from family. As we reclaim each other God can kiss us on
the inside. It is important to appreciate what is possible for
each of us, for the whole family, and for our grandchildren.
Then activities can flow from ways of being. Holidays will
be like birthdays for everybody all at once, times to affirm
life.

The importance of holidays lies deep in the human heart.
Birthdays, Christmas, Thanksgiving, Valentine's Day, and
Easter are a little bit like picking a bouquet of roses. We are
drawn into the subtle beauty of the whole group and the
single bud. Both realities touch us. First, each rose is made

up of a circle of petals, clustered around a life-giving center. You are a rose. Each grown child and grandchild is a rose. Each life is cause for celebration, gently unfolding its petals in our midst. Then, we gather a bouquet to appreciate the fullness of life. We celebrate holidays to gather ourselves in, to rediscover individuals and family.

Aimee stopped at the mailbox on her way in from Junior High. It was the day before her thirteenth birthday. Her mother watched her excitement as she brought in several cards; but then her face fell. Aimee tossed them on the kitchen table in a tirade. "Nobody remembers my birthday!" she announced. This was puzzling. Mother glanced over the envelopes and understood her feelings of rejection. There was no card from Grandpa. He was her last grandparent. Even though he suffered from a disease that made his health unpredictable, still Aimee had hoped. After all, Grandpa did go to the store once a week. Aimee's disappointment created an opportunity for mother and daughter to share their expectations, and to tell God how they felt.

Aimee's life is like that rose: each year is like a new petal, revealing who she is for us and for the world. She needs us. When we notice the years of her life, she can appreciate them more clearly. She needs to be cherished by her whole family in some concrete way.

My survey of thirty grandparents asked people to consider different ways that grandparents might reach out to children. The list included: telephone calls, visits, birthday gifts and cards, worship together, and sharing memories. Each activity could be rated as: always, often, seldom, or never experienced. The one that received the highest rating was giving birthday gifts and cards. Twenty-seven people always gave them, and three often did. It is the celebration of the single rose, the unique life that is at the heart of our holidays and our grandparenting.

Clustered Together

Roses can be clustered together in a broader, more glorious circle of life upon life, shouting out the splendor of a creator's beauty and power. At holidays we feel the urge to gather, putting all our roses into the center of the table that is family. We share life, and our needs get tangled up with our loved one's needs.

There is a classic children's story called *The Little Prince* by Antoine de Saint Exupéry, which describes this phenomenon. The little prince is having difficulties with a pet rose. He finds a fox who teaches him how to establish ties and be "tamed." The two meet each afternoon at four and become friends. The time and attention spent make them important and unique for one another. When they say good-bye the fox says: "It is only with the heart that one can see rightly; what is essential is invisible to the eye."[3]

It is this invisible reality that we hope to experience together. Our efforts to celebrate and nurture are meant to declare, "You are important to me." Our words and actions can give flesh to changing but life-long ties. Our love can also reflect God's primary ties to each of us. Did you ever marvel at the unique beauty of a newborn baby? It is an important blessing to fill our eyes with such a tiny person. It seems like a waste when the child is put to bed where no one can see. But someone does see. Our Father-God delights in each of us, infant or adult. God wants to look and touch and bind himself to us. We are always newborn. Why? God whispers the answer, "Because you are precious in my eyes, because you are honored and I love you" (Isa. 43:4).

How can we reflect this love to our grandchildren? How can we allow ourselves to be "tamed" by the changing relationships in our families? Is each grown child and grandchild beautiful to us? Do we appreciate their splendor in God's sight? Do the activities we plan for holidays flow from this vision?

We want to come together for the holidays that let us claim

each other as family. An important first step in the process is realizing that holidays build upon one another, creating a single event that we enter into each year. We don't have to expect perfection *this Christmas!* The painful times may short-circuit the joy, challenging us to go more deeply to the core of meaning in the holiday. Perhaps at times like this the roses become a deeper red, but they can still flourish.

The Hebrew people, who are at the foundation of our Christian faith, cultivated an appreciation of time as unfolding. Covenant and Passover were events that flowed from God's nature and outlook. Celebrating the Passover from Egypt to the Promised Land was not merely an exercise in conjuring up the past. It was a reality for a people to relive and be immersed in. Families would dress for travel, expecting God to lead them once again.

Circles of Life

The holiday itself is meant to be the celebration of a circle of life, the passing of another year, the movement of the seasons. Winter turns to spring and fall. Also, in our spiritual lives there is the movement and inner circles of feast days. Advent leads to Christmas, then Epiphany. Lent yields Easter. Pentecost blossoms into a month of Sundays. Finally, there is the ultimate journey from life to death to life. Each of these circles is at the basis of our human experience, and can give depth to our holidays.

> The core of a celebration speaks to the hearts of all mankind —in all times and in all places. It speaks the symbolic language of the soul and is hardly ever practical but more poetic, playful, prayerful. All good ceremony asks us to engage and make real the problem at hand and to feel and express fully...its joy and its fear or pain. Ceremony makes the ordinary extraordinary.[4]

One grandfather wanted to share the paradox of Advent and Christmas. He was raised in a family that embraced the waiting as part of the holiday. When he was a child the Christmas tree appeared on Christmas morning. His own grandfather gave gifts only on the Feast of the Magi. So at Thanksgiving time Grandpa brought an Advent calendar. Michael was delighted by the secret windows. He begged and teased to open them. "I can't wait!" was his desperate argument.

Grandpa had anticipated the dilemma. "Then you need help," he exclaimed. "I have another gift," he said as he drew a small package from his pocket. Michael opened it and found an old plastic wheel from a toy truck. Now the boy was really exasperated. "What good will this do?" he asked. This was Grandpa's chance to get to the meaning of Advent. He and Michael sat together. Grandpa turned the wheel in his hand, then in Michael's hand, and told him about ancient times when their ancestors took the wheels off wagons for the winter and brought them in the house. Farmers decorated them with greenery and lights to celebrate the wait until spring. The pair talked about all the things they were waiting for. Grandpa suggested that Michael leave the wheel next to the Advent calendar. When he felt like opening a window ahead of time, he could spin the wheel instead.

We sense the timeless truth of certain events. Baby food companies and hospitals give prizes for the first child born on New Year's Day, not because it's a cute coincidence, but because of the reality of new life. Young lovers propose marriage on Valentine's Day. Mother's Day is one of the busiest days of the year for the telephone companies. Why? The nature of the mother-child relationship is a physical connectedness.

My own experience of a holiday as a circular reality is very clear when I think about summer vacation. For me it means a trip to the ocean. I experience a peace and freedom just watching the blue-green water surge into living crests, then calm itself into shimmering pools. But there have been trips that were frustrating. I married a man who gets sun stroke like most other people tan. In the early years of our marriage we also had preschoolers in tow. An outing at the seashore often lasted only one hour, after a two-hour drive. When I talked out my frustration in the presence of Jesus, I learned something valuable about holidays.

There are layers of joy that make the ocean what it is for me. As a child I enjoyed the chance to walk alone, a rare treat as the oldest of six. I enjoyed floating in the salt water. It gave me a boost as a poor swimmer. I grew to love Sand Hill Cove in Rhode Island, where my father was stationed during World War II, and where his young bride came to visit him. Sometimes we went with caravans of cars driven by uncles and grandparents. All these experiences shaped my expectations. No one trip would match the wealth of all this living, but each could add to the circle. We too can experience layers of meaning and enjoyment with our grandchildren. We can let them piggy-back on our holiday experiences and discover their own.

Welcome Home

As flesh-and-blood human creatures we need a physical place to gather ourselves, our families, and all of our holiday expectations. We look for a comfortable spot to step back from daily life and ordinary times. We may choose restaurants, church halls, houses, city parks, or even just the telephone. No matter where we gather, there is a strong need to experience "home" on important holidays. We must explore this need in order to offer the fullness of meaning that holidays can have for our grandchildren and our families. Each of us has a very personal definition of home that is interwoven with the lives of our loved ones. We must also find ways to become "home" for one another.

The desire to come together at home can be the source of a lot of conflicting expectations. Families, by their very nature, are always growing out of homes. No one building can contain us for very long. The good news is that grandparents often function as a focal point for the extended family: for grown children, their spouses, grandchildren, and even a few stray aunts, uncles. Some grandparents can provide the real opportunity for a family reunion, if circumstances allow. Families without grandparents are bereft of the family homestead, in a very emotional sense. They must search for a substitute.

Families who have such reunions struggle too, usually for clarity of expectations as membership and needs change. This is even more difficult if the matter is not discussed openly. Imagine the consternation of a newly married couple when they come up against mixed expectations. The young husband knows that the Miller family expects to see each other on Thanksgiving Day. It is the only time all year that everyone makes an effort to be together. It just happened that way. His wife is instinctively certain that her family has its reunion on Thanksgiving Day, four hundred miles away. What do they do? Which family do they "belong" to?

If a reunion is not possible, perhaps you can dream aloud with the grown child you are closest to. Be honest about your desires and see if several family members can generate some realistic options. Perhaps a different holiday might work, or a reunion scheduled around a visit from the most distant relative. Adults who grew up together are natural companions at holiday gatherings.

The old song about going over the river and through the woods to grandmother's house for a holiday says more than we think. It raises the deeper issues of hospitality and nurturing. We want to welcome family. It is a part of who we are, even if it happens only once every four years. It is a part of our identity as parents. Seeing children and grandchildren brings our whole lives into a kind of unity.

When our young family visited my grandmother in the nursing home, it was very important that we sit in the big living room together. She could "entertain" us better, offering magazines and space for the children. She went without jelly on her toast for a week in order to give the toddlers a treat to bring home. Sharing her own life stories with John and me was another gift of hospitality. The little ones called our monthly visits "Memere Yumm Sunday." We thought it was because they couldn't pronounce Young, but the holiday name persisted long past the age of faulty diction.

Hospitality of the Heart

Whether or not we can offer our homes, we can always offer our hearts. We can celebrate the ways each grandchild has become an important part of our lives. One grandmother told us that Halloween means Christopher. That's his birthday. Whatever else is involved is secondary, a convenient theme for Chris's birthday party. In our family we have a teenager who was born on Christmas Eve and a child who was an "Epiphany present" born on January 5. We enjoy these two as part of our holiday. It is hard to remember that they would sometimes like celebrations of their own, "like normal people," according to our daughter Mary.

Often grandparents must alter their routines and even living space in order to provide a hospitality of the heart first. If there are toddlers involved, a living room must be made "baby-proof" with breakables, papers, and dangerous objects put out of reach. A room that is not safe only leaves everyone with frazzled tempers, unable to appreciate anything. The bathroom may need some attention also. The National Safety Council reports that 17 percent of all prescription drugs ingested by children belong to their grandparents.

If we take the time to think about the needs of older children, we might be able to get magazines, videos, or books from a local library. We can plan a short project like cleaning a top shelf or labeling a photo album, if the visit will be for a whole day. Remember, we are hoping to welcome family into our lives in some way, not just entertain.

One grandfather was excited about preparing Easter dinner. It had been three years since the family had celebrated it together. Even though there would be only eleven people at the meal, he had cooked a twenty-pound turkey, a ten-pound ham, fifteen potatoes, three vegetables, and four pies. He wasn't sure if there would be enough, but he was taking care of his children again for a few glorious hours.

Some grandparents want to experience holidays in their own homes with family gathered around. It is a chance to see the fruit of so many years' labor. This expectation can also have other needs behind it. It is important to acknowledge these needs. Perhaps we can ask ourselves a few questions to see what is happening in our hearts. How often do we see our grown children? Are needs for regular communication being taken care of on a day-to-day and month-to-month basis? If not, then emotions can be exaggerated, and hospitality of the heart can seem like an impossible goal. Are there external limits on our relationships, such as distance, finances, or occupation, that make visiting difficult? Is the gift of hospitality a difficult one to exercise because of age, illness, or family size? Questions like these aren't meant to discourage us, but to help clarify needs and generate solutions. No family stands still. There is an ebb and flow of members and commitments. If we can welcome the transitions that holidays demand, we can enjoy each other and be instruments of God's love.

Betty and Jim had moved to a small apartment. They didn't have room for a Christmas tree any more. Both of them were depressed about the situation. They enjoyed gathering their two sons and their families around the tree to sing carols each year. A neighbor offered a solution. Two weeks before Christmas Jim and Betty took out all the tree ornaments and decorations. They made four piles, one for their son Larry, one for Robert's family, one pile to keep, and one for the Salvation Army. They put little notes on certain items. "Larry made this in first grade." Another one read, "Aunt Hattie gave us this." The things they kept could be nestled in a spray of greenery on the coffee table, around a tiny tree. There would still be a central place for singing carols. Jim and Betty were able to listen to their own hearts with God's help. They took the time to thank God for the experiences behind each ornament. They laughed when they remembered the time Larry bit into a red bulb and they rushed him to the hospital, only to discover the rest of the ornament behind the couch. Betty cried when they held bits of pink garland that Jim's mother gave them the year they were married.

Some grandparents spend holidays visiting their children's houses. The challenge in this case is accepting someone else's hospitality on the other's terms. Grandparents may feel disoriented by being on unfamiliar territory. (Bring home with you by packing the family photo album.) The emotional work involved can yield advantages. There is the opportunity to experience the tone of family life and the freedom to appreciate individual interests, without responsibility for playing host or hostess. During this kind of visit, there is time to look at a child's room, or listen to a teenager's music, or read a bedtime story. Grandparents can ask and watch. A visit can provide time to be a companion in the ordinary movements of life. Grandparents might alleviate some of the pressure of having an extra "parent" around by taking a daily rest or break alone. One girl, asked about grandpa's whereabouts when her father got home, answered, "Oh, he's taking a nap. Now we can all rest."

Sanctuary-Building

Some families decide that the most important part of their holiday celebration is being together. So they invent ways to overcome limitations and experience home. One couple entertains fourteen children and grandchildren for three days. Most of them sleep on the floor. Every one has a job while at grandma's and grandpa's. Everyone contributes money for groceries.

If anything like this happens at your house, it is good to realize that you are doing more than visiting. Community- and family-building is a part of your holiday. You provide a real service by letting everyone take some responsibility for what happens. This makes for a richer experience. You won't be much fun if you are exhausted from all the preparations. Worse yet, such heroics can make others feel guilty. There will be too much emphasis on getting things done, instead of on being together, which is the heart of hospitality.

When grown children come back to visit, home is more than the place where parents live. It is a haven of their own rootedness, but also a reminder of unhealed and broken bits in their past lives. Even certain objects used at holidays can illicit mixed feelings. Past family experiences shape feelings about the house and about seeing parents. John didn't like seeing his father's empty recliner and the walking stick that hung in the cellar-way for six years after his father's death. On the other hand, Susan grinned each time she walked past a clump of bushes by the side door where she used to play house and tea party. Perhaps we might want to ask them, "What are the hardest and best parts about coming home?"

Each grandchild eavesdrops on parents leftover joys and anxieties about the trip back, picking up a taste of Grandma and Grandpa's home and lives before they even walk in the door. Dan would announce a litany of rules as they walked down his parents' driveway. "Take your shoes off and leave them on the rug. Don't bring food out of the kitchen. And whatever you do, don't ask Grandpa about his hearing aid!" Of course, all of this can serve as a mysterious challenge to grandchildren. Then they may explore these forbidden items for themselves. Grandparent and child can be left to their own devices in order to renegotiate all this.

As our relationships with our grandchildren grow they can experience our homes as "feeling places." Certain rooms get tangled up in our personal love for them. Grandma's kitchen becomes a part of how she nurtures and cares for youngsters. Lisa knows that Poppa buys Tootsie Rolls and keeps them in the yellow cannister. Fred knows that he will sit on the "step-stool-chair" that is kept beside the stove.

Grandma can provide an experience of work, play, and

caring relationships that is filled with meaning, just by helping grandchildren act out what they are already experiencing
in these environments. A little one can sit on grandma's lap
for a moment, then call everyone to the table. Individual
children can help prepare a meal, even taking home a hand-
written copy of a recipe that was used. Perhaps all the love
we associate with kitchens makes us feel more comfortable
sitting at the table for a visit. It's a feeling place where we
are taken care of.

Grandpas have different places tied up with their roles as
mentor, storyteller, or "fixer-upper." David realizes that his
domain with his grandchildren is the cellar and the backyard.
Tom's is the den where he keeps his books and his hunting
trophies. It is good for grandfathers to invite their youngsters to spend a few minutes with them in their own feeling
places. Individual attention can build and heal children in
these settings.

Religious Environment

Because of the nature of family community, our homes can
also provide grandchildren with an experience of their deepest origins and final destiny. A gift of self-discovery can take
on religious significance. Perhaps they will see photos of
themselves as infants or their greeting cards posted on the
refrigerator or mantle. Some grandchildren find a familiar
toy at Gram's house, not to own, but to enjoy when they
visit. Timothy's grandfather keeps a pirate ship in the living
room. Sarah is intrigued by her great-grandma's photo. The
experience is like looking in a mirror.

Grandparents' homes are usually less active than a grandchild's home and can often provide quiet space, where children can experience solitude and even meet God. There may
be rules, such as "No television in the afternoon" that foster such opportunities. Grandma Sally and Grandpa Brian
have a prayer corner in their house. One part of the living
room has a table with a Bible placed carefully on it. A picture

of Jesus hangs on the wall nearby. They each sit there for a few minutes every day and invite older grandchildren to do the same. When children see us using space to worship God they are evangelized. Great-grandmother's rocker with the rosary beads hanging on the arm said a lot to me as a child. She liked to talk to Jesus. He was her friend. He was important. No matter what else was happening at 9 A.M., it was time to stop and pray.

When Jesus is a part of our daily lives we make room for him, just as we do for other loved ones. Then it is only natural that he be a part of our holidays as well. Aren't most holidays based on God's saving action in history? Do we believe that Jesus cares about all the pains and limits of family life that we face during holidays? Do we invite him in too?

Children notice what means the most in our lives. Things we spend a lot of time and effort doing take on a higher priority. In the eyes of little children, they become our religion. If there is a radio, television, and non-stop conversation at all times, what do you suppose we are saying? If children hear us complain about physical illnesses and dead family members, without hope, what will they learn? On the other hand our own efforts to find God can bring fresh meaning to holidays. One grandmother experienced a new conversion through a decision to go to daily Mass. It was only natural for her to place a Paschal candle on the center of her Easter table.

Ritual and Religious Experience

What we do on holidays is just as important as where we share them. Our rituals and actions should be based on primary activities that we enjoy all year. Let me explain. We eat every day, but on holidays we *eat!* Food is a part of the fun. We may experience daily fears, but on Halloween we can celebrate *fears* and bring them to God. We experience death in a family, perhaps through a spouse, a friend, or a pet. But on Easter we experience death with all the stuffings kicked out of it. We underline our daily life through holiday rituals.

The making of a ritual is a creative act fundamental in human life. It is also a divine gesture. Through rituals and ceremonies we people in turn make order out of chaos. In endless space we create a fixed point to orient ourselves: a sacred space. To timelessness we impose rhythmic repetitions: the recurrent feast. And to untamed or unbounded matter, we give a shape, a name, a meaning.[5]

When we celebrate holidays, using the good tablecloth, coloring eggs, carving the turkey, or holding hands to say grace are not frivolous activities. They are the business at hand. Actions give voice to beliefs and relationships.

Catherine gathers her grandchildren at her house for the feast of St. Nicholas on December 6. She tells them the story about Nicholas and how much he loved Jesus, pointing out the connection between the saint and Santa Claus. Catherine's nephew appears in a red suit to give out little gifts. To top off the evening they take out the nativity set and place the characters in it, except for the baby Jesus. He is ceremoniously placed in a drawer. Then the children talk about what birthday gifts they will give Jesus, when they come back on Christmas Eve to put the baby in the manger.

Once four-year-old Jennifer was visiting friends who displayed a manger complete with infant during the Advent season. "Baby Jesus isn't supposed to be there!" she whispered to her mother. "He won't be able to have a birthday party!" Catherine had taught Jennifer a lot about the meaning of Christmas through this little ritual.

Rituals express a deeper reality. That's why they can be so joyous, or so painful. My two-year-old enjoys the "good-bye" ritual at our house. After everyone is off to school or work, she picks up a tiny case full of blocks, waves at me, then gives a kiss and laughs. I miss a similar ritual practiced by my mother-in-law. When we left her house she would give each person a hug and follow us down the driveway. Then she would stand and

talk at the car door until we were seated. Once my oldest daughter took a photo of Mum at the car door. It's my
favorite.

Our daily human rituals are elevated to still another level
when we come together as Christians. Objects and actions
take on a symbolic quality that can either nurture or hinder
our faith in God. An object like a crucifix will trigger off an
avalanche of feelings and associations only if we have experienced it together in our homes and hearts. Our family adds
a piece of purple construction paper behind each cross during Lent. On Good Friday we place a cross in the center of
our table. For Easter week we replace the purple backdrops
with gold paper.

The abstracts of our faith must take on a physical reality in
order to shape our hearts as well. Each liturgical holiday often
relies on a physical symbol that we can use in our homes. For
example, Easter celebrates the Paschal Lamb who is Jesus.
Children can help with drawings of lambs or by picking out
a story about a lamb to read at table. Psalm 23 is so popular
because it allows our imaginations to dwell on this one very
moving symbol.

According to one translation, our shepherd, Jesus, leads
us beside still waters. Did you know that sheep will not drink
from fast, moving water? Also, if they should fall in a rapidly
running brook they are in grave danger? Saturated wool
makes it impossible for them to right themselves. Then they
are prey to drowning and predators. In the same way, God
protects us from dangers that would snatch us from God's
love. Easter is God's ultimate triumph and our protection.

Play and ceremony are very closely related to one another.
When we allow our imaginations to explore the meaning
of God's word to us though images, we get to try on our
faith in new ways. One grandmother has given each of her
children's families a cross depicting the resurrected Jesus.
Easter is deeply ingrained in her own spirituality. She enjoys including her grandchildren in simple morning prayers
before a cross. A few of the grandchildren were very sur-

prised when they realized that crucifixes at church hold a naked, dying Jesus. "Where did they put his clothes?" these grandchildren wanted to know.

There are also times for letting go of religious symbols and rituals, paring down to the essentials. We may need less activity and curtailment of even religious objects as we get older. One grandmother, Rita, was very depressed that she couldn't get to Mass any more. She watched Sunday liturgies on television and received the Eucharist in her home, but was still upset. Then Rita's family came up with a solution. They took a good photograph of the altar in Rita's parish and had a large print made to hang in the living room. She was at home again. On holidays they sit with her and read a psalm together.

It is best to choose religious traditions from childhood, from the growing years in our own families, or from ethnic traditions. Then levels of meaning are already underneath our actions. When this is not possible don't be afraid to add a new ritual, especially if it is geared toward grandchildren. There is something about the child in each of us that will lend an attentive ear and be touched by God. Just explain yourself and the new activity in terms of your own needs to share.

What we do together on holidays serves as an arrangement for the bouquet that is our family. Each generation joins in, according to daily experiences and issues. One family therapist suggests that we eat holiday meals without segregating people at tables by age. We must find ways to bring the roses of our lives together. One life is a bud, closed up and ready to start, another spreading itself full-wide in the daylight, another bending to rest. We can welcome each other with listening hearts. We can provide feeling places. We can acknowledge the source of our days, and our cycles. All of us grow as we draw sustenance from the one vine, Jesus. We can celebrate holidays through rituals that make Jesus our home. Perhaps no one will ever notice the faith underneath our holidays. Perhaps it will be anticlimactic after all the visiting and cakes and presents. But then who knows what our grandchildren will tell their grandchildren when asked what Christmas and Easter are all about?

➤ ○ ➤

For Reflection, Sharing, and Discussion

1. How do you exercise the gift of hospitality toward your family? What do you enjoy most about time spent together? What restrictions limit your ability to welcome them?

2. What holiday rituals were the most meaningful in your growing family's past? How could you continue them now, or share their meaning with your family?

3. What is your dream of an enjoyable family reunion? Who would be present? Where would you gather? What would you enjoy doing? How does your dream coincide or differ from other family members' expectations?

4. Make a map of your house or apartment with a grandchild. Ask him/her to put a mark where they like to find you, then your spouse. Ask about favorite places, and awful places. Mark a spot where each of you might find Jesus.

Activities for Holidays

Christmas

1. Write a waiting litany for meal prayers during Advent.
   Examples:
   We wait for snow to ski . . . Come Lord Jesus.
   Grandpa is waiting to retire . . . Come Lord Jesus.

2. Use a Nativity set to re-enact the Christmas story. Move the figures each week, adding Jesus on Christmas with a

birthday party. Let children place tiny gifts in the manger or snowflakes in the sky above.

3. Make an Advent wreath out of bread dough and decorate it.

Easter

1. Make a set of stations of the cross with a grandchild. Pick out six favorite ones to draw (perhaps after touring a church). Collages of magazine pictures, or silhouettes made by tracing stations in a prayerbook are good too.

2. Try an Easter egg hunt with plastic eggs filled with candy and Scripture verses appropriate to all ages.

3. Make a caterpillar by putting features on a rounded clothespin. Place it in an envelope cocoon at the beginning of Lent. Keep it in your prayer corner until Easter. Then surprise the children by adding wings, with glitter or stars, and carefully repositioning it in the cocoon.

Pentecost

Celebrate Pentecost, the church's birthday, by drawing some large birthday candles decorated with a favorite Christian symbol. Glue children's candles on a cake drawing.

For more holiday suggestions read *To Dance with God* by Gertrud Mueller Nelson (Paulist Press: New York/Mahwah, N.J., 1986).

CHAPTER 3

Loving My Children's Children

G RANDPARENTING MEANS BUILDING BRIDGES across three generations. In Carolyn's life this is a very dramatic reality. When she visits her daughter's family in Puerto Rico, the four-room cottage hums with activity. The four little girls get most excited about seeing the docks and their grandmother's ship. At the end of one of Carolyn's trips, Vanessa reached under the mattress of the bed she shares with her sisters and retrieved a scrap of red paper carefully torn in the shape of a Valentine. She gave it to her grandmother and beamed in response to hugs and kisses. Then Carolyn handed the little card to her daughter and whispered, "What does it say?"

"Oh, it's beautiful mother!" was the reply.

> *Abuela* [Grandmother], . . . I know you only a little. But you are so good to me. I can feel you loving me, and I will never erase you from my heart.
>
> Love, Vanessa

The little Valentine and the visit are still beautiful now that Carolyn is back home. She has experienced the strength of a grandparent's love from two directions. When she was a child, Carolyn shared a bedroom with her French-speaking grandmother. It was hard work to communicate, but they managed, especially when she would help comb Memere's long white hair at night. And now, many years later, she has a grandchild who speaks only Spanish. "Isn't that great," she concludes. "I can be close to Vanessa, like I was to Memere, with a little work and a lot of love." When Carolyn has family gatherings, she includes a cake with flags. The French flag represents her mother's people; the Puerto Rican one, some of her grandchildren; and the Scottish flag flies for her second husband and his grandchildren. "We are a regular United Nations!" she explains.

Grandparents can bridge two different worlds when they choose to develop relationships with their children's children. Travel, translation, and special effort are necessary for some. But in every case bridge-building is involved. Our grandchildren are someone else's babies, born into a world and an era that is not quite ours. They are not being raised in our image. Even if a grandchild occupies "the little room at the top of the stairs," we must be careful to respect the distance between us in order to travel it successfully.

A four-year-old knows that bridge-building is a delicious art form, precisely because of the danger and the possibilities. Tim has a set of wooden blocks that he stacks into a solid wall. Then he takes a ruler and pushes out the blocks in the center, at the base of his structure. Each time he holds his breath, then squeals with delight if the new bridge holds firm. If it collapses, then he laughs and calmly resumes his task.

We can delight in the bridge work involved in relating to our grandchildren. A bridge is firmly anchored on two shores. It holds fast and so do we. Through grandparenting we cherish our families, holding on for dear life. A successful bridge also spans an open area with a great deal of flexibility. In the same way grandparents can guard important breathing and growing space between the generations. A bridge relies on the natural tension of its building materials. We must accept midlife and family tensions as part of our experience, relying on the power of God's love. Finally, the goal of a bridge is the communication it allows. We can enjoy the same goal as we reach out across the generations.

Hang On for Dear Life

My husband gave me a book as a birthday gift last year. It was called *Every Cliché in the Book* by Peggy Rosenthal and George Dardess. Some of our experiences in building family are described in these strange little word-pictures, which we pass on because of their emotional resonance. A most important reality as far as parenting goes is expressed in the adages, "Hang on for dear life!" and "Let's stick together."

Remember what it was like to hold your first new baby? The little squirming softness and the tiny wrinkled face called forth a reaction of heart, mind, and arms. You held on to give life. Now imagine just how many times we have lifted any one of our children from a crib, a play pen, a high chair, or a car seat? If we calculated the minimum as five times a day for three years that would be 5,375 times. With every gesture we made that simple connection of bodies and hearts. A bonding took place, as firm as the steel pilings that anchor a bridge. That bond is still very real, although reshaped and more invisible, after our children become adults. Then later we fall in love all over again as grandparents.

When Pat's daughter Elizabeth announced that she was pregnant, Pat experienced a strange mixture of happiness and depression. She was acutely aware of how much each family member meant to her, because another daughter had been killed in a car accident a few years earlier. Now there would be a new baby to hold; but she wouldn't be able to spend as much time as she would like with Elizabeth and her grandchild, because of her job. Pat talked over her feelings with her husband and decided to quit her job. Cherishing and serving her family took on the importance of a vocation from God. She did not return to work for several years. She knew how fortunate she was to have had such an opportunity.

There is a desire to nurture that is reawakened as a part of our grandparenting. It can be lived out in a variety of ways as the years go by. It is a call to love and create, from a different perspective than when we were just parents. Dick prayed daily for his new grandchild from the beginning of Carol's pregnancy. Two months later he was awakened from a sound sleep with an urgent desire to give this child to God. So he climbed out of bed and prayed for an hour, then went back to sleep. Since it was such an unusual experience he called his son the next day, only to discover that the young couple had experienced a miscarriage. Dick had helped them through it from a distance.

Our desire to cherish grandchildren is a gift that can flourish despite all kinds of obstacles. When I asked Mary how many grandchildren she had, she replied, "Eighteen naturally, and then there is my son-in-law's four kids. I fell in love with them when I met them! They don't call me Gram, but we have a special relationship. My husband and I fill in the spot left by their other set of grandparents who died."

Many grandparents have had the complicated experience of trying to love a grandchild conceived out of wedlock. Others have faced the emotional turmoil of accepting handicaps such as Down's Syndrome. Many have been unsure of their role after grown children are divorced and grandchildren removed from their lives. Some must learn how to be grandparents as they go along because of their own broken childhood.

Some of these difficulties will catapult us into crisis grandparenting. We must find ways to hang on to our families, ways that give assurance but are not counterproductive. For now, we will focus on the bridge-building that is the foundation of any style of spiritual grandparenting. In the last chapter we will consider crises that test our primary way of relating to our families.

When the desire to love and nurture is thwarted we are perched on the edge of conversion and inner healing. We have a very primary question to ask ourselves. Why are we hanging on to them in the first place? What do we want most for our loved ones? We can let suffering become a teachable moment that will mold our hearts and drive us into the arms of a merciful Father-God. We must learn how to "hang on to Jesus" for dear life. It is God's love that has bound us together.

When I was four months pregnant with Mary, our third child, my mother had surgery for ulcerative colitis. She did not do well and required a second operation. Before that operation we talked about a lot of things, realizing the danger of losing one another. I thanked her for being my mother. We asked each other's forgiveness for all the times we had broken the relationship. We prayed together. Mom stopped our conversation at several points that afternoon, and said, "I love you, Therese." I was getting embarrassed by just how often. I told her so, and her reply was, "You'll need to know." She was right. Mom died three weeks later. I have needed to experience her love many times in the fourteen years since then.

I sometimes grieve Mom's loss as my children's grandmother. But in a real way, she is still loving them. Just last month our two-year-old had infections in both ears. Katie was inconsolable. As I rocked her in the middle of the night, I asked Mom to help Katie concentrate on my hand, rubbing her back. Katie calmed down and fell asleep for a few hours. Her grandmother loves her.

When something undermines our love for children and grandchildren, it makes us stop and take account of inner resources. Let's return to the physical reality of lifting a child. A person can hold only so many children in one lap. That's why people who give birth to more than triplets have our instant sympathy. We know our physical limits.

Hang Loose and Leave Space

When we experience emotional limits and are "at our wit's end," we realize another important part of love. The experience of dangling by emotional threads can help us let go in a healthy way. When my mom died, my grandmother and Aunt Lillie took on the task of grandmothering my children. Aunt Lillie is still on hand at age ninety-six, but has the experience of being at her "wit's end" often. She cannot tolerate being in the same room with a curious toddler for more than thirty minutes. Children have a way of pushing all of us to the brink.

There are many times when we can let go of our families only by giving loved ones to someone else. We may need the support of a spouse, friends, or even professional counselors when things get unraveled. When we receive support from others, we are free to experience the other side of bonding, giving a child or grandchild freedom. We can allow for breathing space in the relationship, like a bridge leaves room for boats and water underneath. We are not God. We cannot manufacture a child's happiness at all cost. Others, even the child, have responsibilities as well.

Ethel's twenty-year-old daughter, Yolanda, was in the Army when she announced that she was pregnant. Ethel was more than furious. She said many things she later regretted. Then she realized it was time to let her unmarried daughter make her own decisions. She worked hard at being a quiet source of strength. When her grandchild was six months old, Ethel became concerned again. Yolanda had not considered baptism. She remembers saying, "This baby is a human being with an inheritance of God's love and a birthright to know the Lord. What will you do about that?" Somehow, she awakened Yolanda's vocation as a mother. Yolanda brought the baby for baptism and has remained faithful to her God in the eight years since. No matter where she is assigned to duty on Sundays, she tells her C.O. she has to get to a Mass.

Ethel's style or language might not be yours, but you will find ways to let go and affirm your grown children. Perhaps a sense of humor is a contribution that you can make when a young family is under pressure. It is a way of letting go. A child who is smearing jelly on the table can be referred to as an artist. A teenage son with long hair can be accepted as the "spitting image" of Great-great-great-great-great-great Grandpa Prouty who fought in the Revolutionary War. People say that Pope John XXIII accomplished much through his sense of humor. When asked how many people worked at the Vatican, he replied, "Well, I guess about half of them."

Letting go is a lot of hard work. For the five thousand times we picked a child up, there are perhaps a thousand times when we must emotionally let go. We must put them in God's hands when they are sick, or leave for school, when they drive cars, or choose spouses and marry. Parents and grandparents often challenge each other to let go without even realizing it. When I was an infant my parents lived with Mom's parents and my Great-grandmother Derosier. That meant there were five people fighting over whose turn it was to hold me in the rocking chair. Five people bonding at once means letting go for four people at a time.

To make matters worse, we are already challenged to let go of our youth, our earning power, our families, and even our hair, eyesight, and figures. Now are we supposed to let go of grandchildren, the one bright new spot in life? The answer is "Yes!" We do so to give life. According to my survey many grandparents realize the suffering involved. They like "not being fully responsible for a grandchild's upbringing"; yet they find it difficult to "stand by and let my children be parents." The experience entails giving up our opinions and a sense of order and control.

Adult Children as Apprentices

Our relationships with our grandchildren are very dependent on our relationships with our grown children. This middle generation acts as the bridge between us in many ways. Their lifestyle, desire to communicate with us, emotional health, and choice of a place to live have a profound effect on our availability as grandparents. Have we accepted them for the unique people they are becoming? Do we respect them as apprentice bridge builders? Do we see all the conditions in their lives as opportunities or as obstacles?

We are the first social audience for grown children as new parents. When Rachel was born my mother came into the hospital room and said, "Congratulations. You have a beautiful daughter." I was shocked. It was the first time I thought of myself as having a daughter. I have since offered grandmotherly support in the supermarket. After a mother has repeated her "No" to a whining child who wants candy, I'll wink at her and say, "You're doing a good job."

We provide the same social support for a young couple. Did you ever approach the bride at a wedding reception and say, "Congratulations, Mrs. Beale?" The look of surprise and excitement is precious. We have said yes to the marriage. When two people live together without contract, no one has placed the relationship out in public. No one is asking for our yes or no. The couple aren't even asking each other for one.

We do our grandchildren a real service when we affirm the parents and family that they are a product of. Claudia was excited about her son and his family moving into the small apartment they had built in their home for Ted's parents years earlier. But Claudia and Ted knew that it would be important to add a separate entrance for the apartment and always knock before entering. They have worked at giving the young family privacy. Claudia was surprised at how much work is involved: even sharing a mailbox means letting go of what she thinks might be happening.

Charles Keating points out the challenge involved in affirming a grown child's family and marriage in his book *Dealing with Difficult People*. He cautions us to support the family as a unit. We must be in touch with all the emotions and expectations behind the way we treat each person in the couple: "There are different perceptions of the couple and of each one of the couple; (2) family 'ties' are significant; (3) pride in a member of the family and expectations of the marriage union are present. . . . These are good reasons since we are not brains on stilts."[6] How do we face the challenge?

Our acceptance can be upbuilding. Our grown children are facing the task of establishing their families and growing in intimacy with one another. If we hold on too tight they will have a more difficult job. We may want to ask ourselves:

Am I in touch with my feelings about them? Do I accept my son- or daughter-in-law? Do I respect their family as more important to them than mine? Do I allow them their own style of married life?

Our young people are also testing themselves as individuals to find out where they can get a firm footing. They are choosing their own "shoulds" to live by. If we are unsupportive, it becomes a painful reminder of their own uncertainties. Religious beliefs must also go through a kind of purification some time in early adulthood. Some go through a temporary or permanent "vacation" from religious traditions during the search. Our confidence in them will give witness to God's love as unshakable. "Remaining steadfast in faith while children grow away is crucial to both parents' and children's well-being. If we parents allow their disaffection to shake our faith, it tells our kids that we practice spirituality more for their sake than ours."[7]

Midlife Tension in the Bridge

There is pleasure and pain in facing change in ourselves, as well as in our children. When I was a little girl I thought my great-grandmother's face was beautiful, mostly because of her smile and hundreds of wrinkles in her soft skin. Now I am challenged to incorporate my own aging and wrinkles into a changing definition of beauty for myself. There is a disorientation and a shift in the way we define many things midway through life. Events trigger a change in focus. Perhaps a death redefines former goals as unreachable. Maybe inner rules about what makes life important have been reversed. One grandfather struggled with early retirement from business and a second look at marriage. He smiled and said, "Midlife crisis isn't really what we should worry about. We should come to grips with aging; that lasts much longer." He had reached a point of reintegrating his life.

There are limits. We all run out of time. We run out of money. We run out! The material in the bridge becomes strained. It isn't something that happens just to our parents, neighbors, and friends. If you need to understand this process, I would recommend the Faucetts' book in the bibliography.

The things we mourn and must come to grips with are very personal. When my father-in-law was dying in the hospital, each visitor would be greeted by the question, "Did you bring my pants?" He wanted to walk down the hall and out of the building as master of his own destiny. If we answered no, a tirade would follow. So we would say yes. We had confidence in his manhood and in his brother Jesus who would come to walk down the hall and out into the Sun with him.

After her husband's death, Sylvia began to nag her grown children, "Nobody ever visits me!" She missed the committed and dependable relationship she enjoyed with her spouse. Without realizing it, she was expecting them to take his place. Some were able to establish agreements with her that she could rely on. One daughter committed herself to weekly shopping errands. One promised to visit twice a year and write every three weeks. Others avoided her or made promises that were unrealistic. Sylvia was unable to face the tensions and mourning that were a part of her own midlife adjustment, so parent-child relationships were strained.

Many grandparents experience a sense of loss as they remember the growing years of family life. One grandmother told me that when she is feeling down, the worst place for her to be is in the children's old bedrooms. If she goes there, she begins to cry. Her life isn't as full or rich with people's needs and activities. Grandchildren don't fill the same kind of spot in her heart.

The tension between "what is" and "what was" is an essential ingredient of spiritual grandparenting. As we feel ourselves torn in opposite directions, we experience what bridge builders call tensile strength. Life is fragile. The stretching we experience is a new invitation to faith. Our hope can become the presence of Jesus uniting all time, giving rootedness and purpose. If we resist such a task, then our strength as spiritual grandparents is sapped.

Janet's twins were ten years old when her son's first child was born. She was not interested in being a grandmother. It is only now, eight years later, that she would like to work on closer relationships with her four grandchildren, but it will be much more difficult for them now.

A willingness to deal with issues of inner acceptance empowers us with a new objectivity in relating to grown children. Rose told me that she prays for "careful prudence," which according to Webster's dictionary means the ability to look ahead and "discipline oneself according to the use of reason." She used to give grandchildren religious books, but noticed that they weren't being read, so she stopped. Arthur confessed that it is hard for him to "stand aside and let his children parent." He disagrees about some things like spanking, eating habits, and bedtime. Sometimes it is best for him to leave the room for a moment and deal with himself first.

As we yield to the gift of prudence, we give ourselves time to learn several important things. First, if we act on impulse we may not be offering the model of self-discipline that we espouse. We can take the opportunity to learn about ourselves. Second, we may be repeating a similar pattern of disagreement we have with a spouse. One grandmother told me her favorite part of grandparenting is "spoiling" the children. Her husband told me the hardest part of grandparenting is "not spoiling" them. Third, we must sort out major and minor differences in parenting. Of course we will have opinions. We have been parents for a long time. One mother said she still has teeth marks on her tongue from resisting the urge to tell her children what was "wrong."

The majority of our differences are minor questions of style and personality. Major differences must be tested in terms of the personal safety of our grandchildren and serious unmet needs in their parents. If these are at stake, then we are involved in crisis grandparenting. Finally, remember this. We have already had twenty years of input in the way our children define discipline and parenting. It is important to let them assimilate that much first.

Family Tensions

Some of the tensions between us can be almost laughable. There are so many kinds of personalities in the human community. I recall a sense of alienation from my father-in-law in the early years of our relationship. I can't recall any pleasant conversations back then. Even meals were touchy. If I served an unfamiliar food, he would ask, "What are you trying to do, poison me!" Then a strange thing happened. I gave birth to our son Peter. When we took the boy for a visit, Dad came out of the house and opened the car door for me. I was shocked. What had happened was almost comical. I had given him another grandson, and we had the child in common.

The joy and the curse of family life is that we can't (or at least shouldn't) run away from the wealth of different kinds of personalities in the human community. Dad was actually my grandfather's age and had an old farmer's respect for sturdy sons. He also had undiagnosed food allergies, hence the concern about being poisoned. Worst (or best?) of all, we were both introverts, which makes for difficult conversation under any circumstances. What I had to do after Peter's birth was to find other things we had in common. The same can be done with sons- and daughters-in-law. I discovered that Dad loved nature. So I would begin a visit by admiring the trees he planted in the backyard or inquiring about his garden.

Many people appreciate the Meyers-Briggs theory of four basic personality indicators. A simple explanation of it can be found in Keating's book in the bibliography. The research points toward four sets of traits that each of us has. The particular combination shapes our relationships with others.

We are: *introverts* — most at home in an inner world, OR
extroverts — energized by contact with others.

We are: *sensing* — grounded in physical, present detail, OR
intuitive — dream, idea, and future oriented.

We are: *thinkers* — who live by reason, logic, facts, OR
feelers — geared toward values and harmony.

We are: *perceivers* — interested in what is happening, OR
judgers — needing a system of control and order.

These categories can help us appreciate ourselves. We favor one in each pair, but must deal with the weaker of the two in midlife. We can also appreciate the effect of combinations on relationships. The ideal relationship exists between two people who have two similar as well as two opposite traits. My husband and I balance each other as extrovert and introvert, but are both thinkers. My father-in-law and I had too many traits in common. Combinations affect families. Our poor daughter Mary is the only feeler in a house full of thinkers. She gets frustrated, yet we need her.

We can read the Gospels for a vision of wholeness in communication. Consider the way Jesus respected Zaccheus, the sinful woman, and Nicodemus. Religious leaders chided him for treating women and children as equals, a practice unheard of in his day. Jesus helps us too. In the security of his love we need not cling to our own authority and roles. We can approach our children and even grandchildren as equals. One great-grandmother told me, "My daughter and I are both so old that we are grandmothers together." Another grandmother, Marie, visits part of her family in Florida for a month each spring. She shares a bedroom with two teenage granddaughters. "We become very intimate. There isn't much choice," she laughed. "I hang out at night with the girls and their friends." When we can accept each other as equals, we can report feelings, problems, and needs without trying to solve them or win.

Communication Bridges Generations

When we cultivate good relationships in our families we build a network of bridges, although this is where the image of the bridge may falter. A network of bridges sounds too much like an overgrown freeway system. There is a spot nicknamed "Spaghetti Junction" where several highways intersect and wind around downtown St. Paul, Minnesota. Who wants the chaos associated with that kind of intersection in our personal relationships? Still, there is a point to consider when we look at all that goes on among members of a family. We must ask ourselves what kind of communication we hope for, what standard we measure ourselves by. The Apostle Paul offers a goal:

> This is what I pray, kneeling before the Father, from whom every family, whether spiritual or natural, takes its name:
> Out of his infinite glory, may he give you the power through his Spirit for your hidden self to grow strong, so that Christ may live in our hearts through faith, and then, planted in love and built on love, you will with all the saints have strength to grasp the breadth and the length... until, knowing the love of Christ... you are filled with the utter fullness of God.
> — Ephesians 3:14–19

Jesus reveals himself to us, satisfying our deepest needs and calling us to live by the power of his Spirit. Through him we are free to reveal ourselves to one another. We are empowered to listen also, so that each person's hidden self may grow strong. We need not compete or worry. In Jesus the Christ we are brothers and sisters. Our goal of quality relations and community is based in the model Jesus provides.

Spiritual grandparents can strive to speak God's love, with and without words. I'll let two children explain:

Many a times, I ask my grandmother
To make me understand the things that make me wonder.
Her words are like flowers
That bloom when it showers.
Often times she leaves me with somethings to ponder.

Her expressions reveal through her eyes
Her life is filled with dreams
Just like the rivers and the streams.

Although my grandma is old and gray,
She still has a lot to say.
She is so gentle and kind
Her endless love is our special bind.

— Jason Amplo

My grandfather is really neat,
from his head down to his feet.
Although sometimes he is very stern,
he always shows me his concern.
And though he doesn't always show it,
he really loves me. I just know it!
If you knew him like I do,
you would say, "Oh lucky you!"

— Christopher Lambot

Our goal in communicating is a oneness of heart and mind, not idea, behavior, or emotions. We hope to understand each other. There is freedom in agreeing about the important things and letting the rest go by. This is particularly helpful as we look at the issue of child-rearing.

Grandpa Sam's hobby is keeping pigeons. He's had coops behind his house for more than twenty years. Sam's grandson Matthew likes the birds, unlike any of the generation before him. Sam is delighted. But there is a problem. Matthew's parents are afraid he will get involved with the pigeons that try to roost under the eaves of their own house. So Grandpa Sam has given two birds to Matthew, but keeps them in his coops. It's not the ideal way for him to learn animal care, but unity of purpose and relationships is important to all of them.

Bumpy Bridges

As Christians we can agree to disagree. We can be vulnerable and communicate with Jesus as our safety net. The Wilmers suspected a grave problem with alcohol at Gramma's. Then on one occasion Gramma was actually drunk while baby-sitting Alice and Meagan. The loving thing to do was to confront her. "We were frightened and angry when we came back from the movies and found you drunk. The children felt scared and confused when you were stumbling around and could not respond to them."

When there is a problem we can search for common ground. We can name specific actions and our feelings, as well as concern for consequences. Then there is time for listening and affirming the relationship. In the example above the last step might sound like this. "We are sure you love Meagan and Alice as much as we do and don't want to hurt them. We hope you understand our decision not to leave them alone here until you get regular help with alcohol management. We love you and want to see you well again."

It is often the emotional attachments between us that encourage us to pursue our own healing and growth. Clarence has arthritis in his hands, but he promised his grandson he would teach him to whittle. So they meet every other Friday afternoon. Gifts, and even problems, can become tools for building one another up in Jesus. Pigeons, whittling, and a teenager's bedroom become opportunities for building bridges. Conflicts are normal as different expectations emerge. It is how we handle expectations that matters. Do we use an imaginary hammer to insist on our way and beat others into submission? Do we reach for an imaginary saw to cut off relationships? Do we rely on imaginary pliers to cling to and appease others, avoiding needs that squeeze us? No matter what the temptation we can decide to build bridges, to hang on and let go of others.

Bob had hoped he would have more time with his grand-kids. But instead the grandchildren usually visit during the day while he is at work. "I feel envy. My wife gets all the time with them." But he realizes that he is still a young grandfather, unlike his own grandpa, who was *always* a retired taxi dispatcher. "Maybe later," he thinks aloud. "If I'm still up to the constant chatter.... Maybe later."

We can leave room for later, for the work of staying in touch with grandchildren who live far away. If we view each other as brothers and sisters, we can treat grown children and grandchildren with equal respect. Carol always asks her daughter's permission before taking Mark to church with her.

Tara treats her grandchild with humility but firmness. When she is babysitting and she "does little naughty things," she corrects her with this reminder: "I don't expect you to be perfect. Grandma isn't perfect. I just want you to stop and think about what you are doing, and what Jesus might do if he was here." She has a certain courage that she learned from her own grandparents. When Tara was an infant she was ill and close to death. Her weeping parents had picked out a burial plot. But Grandpaw came along and would hear nothing of their fears. He took her home to Grandmaw and they nursed her back to health, then raised her till she was five.

We all want what is good and holy for our loved ones. We build bridges to accomplish this. We can acknowledge the love and the hurts that have occurred in the process. There are bonds that can sustain us all. There is also an invitation to let go. We need space to grapple with aging. Our children need space to discover their own skills as bridge builders. Jesus will help us affirm and forgive one another. He is God's enduring word of love. When we speak and live that word, the bond between the generations will be "strengthened to grasp the breadth and the length ... until [we] are filled with the utter fullness of God" (Eph. 3:18–19).

≺ ○ ≻

For Reflection, Sharing, and Discussion

1. Picture a favorite bridge. What kind of a bridge is it? What do you like and dislike about bridges? How are you a bridge between different members of your family?

2. Recall the experience of holding your newborn child. What did you most enjoy about the experience? How do you still hold and cherish your children now?

3. When did you first think of yourself as an adult? What events helped you realize that your children are adults? How has this realization changed your relationship with them?

4. Our adult children also build relationships and bridges in their own lives. How do you acknowledge and affirm those relationships? How could you grow in this area?

5. We can respect our children as "apprentice" parents. They have the primary responsibility of raising our grandchildren. What skills have you seen in them? How have you exercised "careful prudence" in watching them parent?

Activities

1. God has given each of your children and grandchildren to you as gift. Try a prayer exercise that places them in God's care. If you have a big family, make a list and choose one each day.

   • Come into the presence of Jesus with a song, a little prayer like the Our Father, or a Scripture reading.

   • Take a moment to picture your child. Some people like to hold a photograph as they pray. See if you can imagine Jesus standing near, smiling, and welcoming this loved one.

- Surrender this person to God, using whatever words are most comfortable. Let go of specific worries. You might read Psalm 23 and substitute your loved one's name.

- Celebrate God's love in some concrete way.

2. Survey how your family views conflict through this exercise. (Keep it light but be willing to do some serious listening.)

A Lot of Things Make My Blood Boil

Ask them to match the following offenses with the rising "temperature" of their blood.

95.6° _____	1. someone spills food on the floor
105° _____	2. someone interrupts my talking
139° _____	3. someone forgets my birthday
172° _____	4. whining and complaining
212° _____	5. someone giving me orders

Ask: If you felt like fighting and there were only imaginary tools nearby, would you grab

_____ saw
_____ hammer
_____ pliers
_____ other

Compare your answers to these two exercises in order to see what you have in common. Listen for *feelings* and reasons.

CHAPTER 4

History-Building through Story

O NCE UPON A TIME, when June's paternal grandfather, Henry Silberhorn, was a foreman in charge of stevedores down at the docks in New York City. In the middle of a June night in 1855, some of Henry's men came pounding on his door. His heart and mind raced through all manner of tragedies as he scurried into his pants and out into the front hall.

"Henry! Henry! You've got to come quick!" they urged him. "There's a woman all cut up in pieces and shoved into boxes on a ship down at Pier Seven. You've got to come now!"

Grandpa's worst imaginings took on an even grimmer tone. He followed them off into the night muttering to himself. What would he do? Had the police been called? How would he manage his own stomach in such a gruesome situation? Who had done such a thing? He thought the horses would never get there.

Well, when Henry Silberhorn got to the ship at Pier Seven what he encountered was a woman of some renown who was indeed in several boxes, 214 of them to be exact. She was the Statue of Liberty. What a joke! He guffawed and giggled right along with his crew, till tears came to his eyes.

June doesn't know much else about her grandfather, but perhaps this one little glimpse is just enough. He could laugh at himself and see life as an adventure. That's the punch line. She sees these qualities as worth imitating in her own life, worth passing on for the rest of her family to appreciate.

Grandparents are family historians in the richest sense.

We have had first-hand experiences with people and places that have shaped both family and world. We have a unique point of view on past events. Our souls are pieced together and molded by the things we have lived through and insights we have adopted as our theme songs. As we come to grips with aging we have a broader point of view on generations gone before, and those yet to come. We may experience the urge to summarize and conclude, to divide life into chapters, and to save records.

Where do we start when there is so much to tell? Each of us begins with our own personal story. We reflect, rework, and sort out what has happened to us, and then to important loved ones. Some of us do this out loud; some prefer to do it internally, rather than share with others. Mary Beth was dying in a hospice in Hudson, Wisconsin. Her burning desire was to weave one last story out of all the important things that had happened to her. Her story was pulsating with characters and plot. The climax was at hand. She could take her place in an unknown future only if she knew that what she had learned would endure somehow. A sister volunteered to help Mary Beth tape-record her reflections on the main events in her childhood, marriage, career, and parenting. She ended with feelings about going home to see her husband and her God.

Sharing personal history is an art form that involves a deeply human need and also a creative process. It can embrace facts, stories, diary keeping, genealogy, writing, and oral tradition. An awareness of the process can transform the raw materials of memory, fact, and stories into vital tools for the spiritual grandparent.

First we will examine the nature of this creative process. Then we will explore the value of our personal history in grandchildren's lives. Next we will outline a job description for family historians. Finally we will consider ways that spiritual grandparents can help young people continue their own stories into the future.

Humans Are Story Animals

A good storyteller creates a world and invites others to enter. The movement of time through a personal event is highlighted. The emotions and issues underneath that event are celebrated and underlined. Let's return to our opening example about Grandpa Silberhorn. It tells us only one event and does not try to explain all that he did at the docks. The story begins with his fear and confusion about an emergency, in the light of his responsibilities. Finally, it involves us, stirring up emotions. Ethel Barrett explains these essential ingredients in her practical book about storytelling: "The ability to tell a story well is the gift of expression, the gift of interpretation — the ability to take an event from the memory or from the printed page — and make it come to life."[8]

We don't all have famous relatives like Henry. What we do have are past events that have touched us in all sorts of ways, taking on levels of meaning as we look back. Certain personal tales become like important theme songs, or threads to be rewoven. Perhaps other family members can repeat them. Finch children know that Grandpa met Grandma at Northridge Furniture Company. He walked up to her switchboard and remarked, "How come they didn't hire somebody good looking for this job?" Amy's grandmother shared this story with her youngsters:

> At the time, my grandmother had two small boys, my mother's brothers, Francis and Allie. They lived upstairs on a main road. They had a porch in the front that my grandmother would lay the pillows and blankets on, so they could air. One day my mother's brothers thought they would help their mom, by laying her underpants on the porch too. When my grandmother went to look for her underpants, they were gone. After looking around, she noticed them out on the roof.
> — Amy Unetich

The desire to share personal events and history with loved ones is important. We want to be heard and appreciated. This is normal. We want to make a connection of mind and heart through these stories. This is good. If we also share out of a genuine concern for the events and emotions in our grand-children's lives, then another important part of the process occurs. Life quickens in the telling. Unfortunately this con-cern for our audience means some dying to self. We must be willing to look at our lives from their point of view, and to listen in turn, to avoid confusion and boredom.

It can be hard work to find that spot in time and heart when storytelling will bring us closer to our grandchildren. My husband and I began a ritual almost ten years ago to cul-tivate listening and story-sharing. We ask each person what he or she liked about the day's events at the supper table. We encourage more than the reporting of facts. We try to leave the door open for stories that describe a personal response to daily life.

It is also important to understand how children and adults approach storytelling. There is common ground, and there are differences. People of all ages divide reality into manage-able chunks by telling themselves what has happened and what could be. We must appreciate the gift of "storying" as a basic human quality, so we may be more sensitive and effec-tive. We talk things out inside our heads. Event and emotion are welded into a single unit of truth so we can interpret the meaning of life. We have this process in common.

My father likes to tell the story about his dad shaving one stormy morning in the kitchen of their farmhouse in Charlton. Grandpa Fenner had a small mirror perched on the window sill at the time. As he reached down to clean his blade in a bowl of sudsy water, he was struck by lightning and thrown across the kitchen. He survived, and the event took on meaning. It was as if the gift of endurance was re-inforced by the lightning. He had lived this reality before. Grandpa Fenner had lost his father at age seven and was placed in an orphanage. He was retrieved by his mother and her new husband several years later, only to experience re-jection again when he converted to Catholicism. He would later experience the strain of raising twelve children. The last four were born while Grandma had diabetes, a very dangerous condition at the time. She died at age fifty-five. The event in Grandpa Fenner's story was not just being struck by lightning. The event was survival. Harry was jolted by the orphanage, the twelve children, and his wife's illness.

One author describes our desire to find wholeness through story and language. Language is a powerful tool to grasp life and try to share it with others. Anyone who has told a teenager to be home "early" knows that a single word has many meanings and carries much weight. When we string a few words together even the human heart and soul can be built up or torn down.

> Storying is a term created by psychologist Renée Fuller, who maintains that this act is so fundamental to intellectual development that we underestimate its importance. The child's ability to create wholeness out of his or her manifold experience . . . expresses an innate human need to make mental connections, to perceive patterns, to create relationships among people, things, feelings, and events — and to express these perceived connections to others.[9]

Feeling Our Way through Story

We have a human desire to connect different kinds of reality. We share this approach to life with our grandchildren. It is part of what creates oneness between us as storyteller and audience no matter what the age. Of course we have different issues to act out as we move from childhood to adult life. Little ones will imitate experiences like eating, holding, and walking with dolls and Fisher-Price people. Our little Katie sings the same lullaby to her doll that we sing to her at bed time. Older children use Teenage Mutant Ninja Turtles or Barbies to act out what has happened to them at school.

For the child a story is an opportunity to recognize and *name* events and emotions. A little girl might say, "My doll is scared of the dog down the street." A young boy might boast,

"I made ten baskets in gym class!" when he actually made one that he was *very* proud of. Sometimes events, emotions, and details get tangled together. A child explores fantasies through story also. The Star Wars movies were a storytelling breakthrough for children raised in a world threatened by nuclear war. The power of goodness, or "The Force," was stronger than the great evils of technology.

For adults storytelling is a natural way to process everyday life. Think of how important it is to tell others about an engagement, a serious illness, a pregnancy. Listening to ourselves explain details and emotions helps us get our bearings as we experience events. The present moment becomes more important, leaving behind an emphasis on fantasy. Young adults hope to achieve intimacy through the melding of lives and stories. They hope to make a statement, to act out an important inner story and plot.

For grandparents who have faced the transition of midlife, the emerging characters of age and death demand a place in our life's story. Our vision changes. We adopt a new slant and purpose for storytelling. The present becomes a springboard for reworking memories and reorganizing perceptions of time and self. Somehow we cross an invisible border between story and history as our primary focus. It is healthy to keep an ongoing balance between the two, but the past has new potential as a welcomed second home.

As spiritual grandparents, we hope to move freely between past, present, and future. We hope to be comfortable in the world of faith and invite grandchildren to travel with us through history-sharing. Our common ground in sharing stories can be emotions triggered by past, present, and future events. Even though children may put a high priority on the future, and grandparents on the past, we meet when things touch us deeply.

Dorothy's house is a tribute to cleanliness and a bevy of cleaning products. Grandchildren must remove their shoes, help with dishes, and pick up after themselves. A granddaughter asked Dorothy when she first started being so clean. Dorothy winced but volunteered her story. She remembered her parents fighting a lot. Her father was an abusive alcoholic. Her mother would get so angry that she would throw hot cups of tea at him. After a while there were lots of tea-stained splatters on the kitchen walls in her childhood home. At age seven Dorothy vowed that she would allow no such thing in her own life. The house would be clean. Dorothy's freedom in sharing the emotions behind her behavior gave her granddaughter new compassion. The desire to live in peace was something they had in common.

Living Ancestors

Grandparents can be living connections with people from other times and cultures. One Irish grandmother in St. Louis has begun collecting stories and bits of Mexican American history for her granddaughter. She is convinced of the value of this little girl's heritage on both sides of the family. Grandchildren can fall in love with people from history as they absorb a healthy attitude toward the past from us. Of course, this part of grandparenting evolves with the child's age. Groundwork is laid by early cuddling and attention; and then later, physical intimacy can give way to an intimacy of ideas. An openness to history is also built on sharing imaginative play and stories from a child's book. Still, history-sharing is different from reading a story together because it takes an appreciation of time that little children do not have. When children become aware of history, they equate it with a parent or grandparent's life span. There will be questions like "Grandma, what was it like to ride in a covered wagon?" or "Grandpa, did you fight in the Revolutionary War?"

It may seem laughable to realize that small children think we traveled in covered wagons. Yet there is a truth to their outlook. I went to a lecture on French-Canadian heritage that I remember two sentences from, at most. I went to a second presentation about early settlers and fur traders given by a man in costume posing as a *voyageur*, and I remember every word and gesture. Our very person speaks volumes to children. We can provide a living view of important historical events. This is a valuable treasure to hand on to the next generations. We can also offer first-hand insights into other cultures, family background, and personal history. In my survey about 60 percent of the grandparents share memories and stories about the past with a grandchild. There was also a high correlation between feeling close and sharing memories.

Luke's grandfather told him what it was like to be a soldier in World War II. Luke knows about the operations near Okinawa and about dengue fever. His grandfather was discharged on Christmas Eve and excited about the prospects of no more global wars. Luke has learned more than what is in history books. He knows how World War II felt and what it meant back then. This gives him a broader view of life. He is not dependent solely on his time and culture for a definition of peace. The outlook of another generation gives him what is called "social immunity," an independence of thought and values.

Events in our family's history are also important. We can be living representatives of a shared ancestry. Each family needs pieces of oral tradition that help individuals get their bearings. In a world that changes so fast, we also need experiences that create a sense of belonging. Family history can be such an experience. The Tremblays can identify with several generations of talented businessmen. William was a blacksmith. His son Joseph opened a brick yard. By 1916, he had twenty horses and $22,000 to show for his efforts. Joseph and his son Louis operated a milk business that thrived until Louis's retirement. He was able to pay cash for a small home with the proceeds from the sale of the business.

Grandparents can offer children a genealogical perspective on their lives. Each is the unique product of scores of families and marriages. We can pass along the bare bones of their biological and social framework. Each child can rummage through all the personalities and traits assembled in their genealogy and fantasize about their own choices as adults. Genealogical information and charts can also put order into our family stories and memories, functioning like a framework.

I became very interested in genealogy when our family moved to the Midwest. I dealt with my uprootedness by learning more about earlier generations. Knowing these ancestors has given me an appreciation for their strength of character. I "met" pre-teens who worked in mills, young mothers who died of diphtheria, a widow whose husband was killed by a dog. There were grandparents who crafted violins, sang at town gatherings, made astronaut suits, built crystal sets, and brewed root beer in the cellar.

Family Biographer

Grandparents have an incredible cast of characters to choose from when sharing family stories. Some may not know about the lives of as many individuals as others; but what counts is our interest and willingness to share. We hold an ace as far as knowledge about important figures goes. Often the kind of family stories that grandchildren enjoy most are the stories about their own parents when they were kids. Grandparents are "official biographers" for those mysterious times when Mom and Dad were real people, real kids, not just "grown-up dult," as one of our children used to say.

Our kids gloated with satisfaction when Memere told them the real truth about their straight-laced father. It seems that when John was a toddler he used to take his shoes off in the snow. Better yet, when he was seven, John and his cousin had their pants nailed to the porch steps. Brother Gerry had discovered them in the barn playing with his chemistry set. Discipline around here has never been quite the same since.

Lest my husband accuse me of airing only his dirty laundry, I should add a confession of my own. Aunt Lillie reassures my independent teens with stories about my attitude as a junior high person experimenting in the kitchen. Even if I was in the midst of a culinary disaster, I would reject her suggestions. "I can do this by myself," was my favorite declaration.

There are good and bad memories that reflect a pattern of personal and family formation. Some grandparents get involved in writing down or tape-recording stories about their own parents and grandparents. Some try to reach back as far as they can for clues to identity, giftedness, and needs. Others reach back to gain compassion for themselves and their loved ones. We may be tempted to dwell on only good memories, or only bad. This is normal, but we do need a willingness to look at both in order to be of real service to our families.

Myrtle was devastated by her grandson Ben's alcoholism. She had been raised by an alcoholic father, and had been very careful to avoid the disease within her marriage and children's lives. She began to ask elderly aunts and uncles about her father's problem. She found out that he had been an immigrant, whose father was also an alcoholic. Myrtle was convinced that the problem would only get worse through silence. She initiated sensitive conversations and story-sharing with her grandson. "He needs to know that he's not alone," she explained. Ben realized the importance of his efforts at sobriety from a new perspective. He had a choice and a little more personal information to add to the picture.

What we choose to share from our personal lives can help build or subvert our relationships with our grandchildren. Everyone has had the experience of listening to an elder recite one event after another, as if reading out of diary that has no page numbers and no beginning or end. This is not generally uplifting or enjoyable. Those of us who are guilty of such practices may want to stop ourselves and admit, "I've said too much. I don't want to stop talking, but I will." Our goal is to capture an important moment in a very personal journey of life. I use the word "journey" very deliberately.

Capturing the Spiritual Journey

What we decide to share carries a wisdom and intimacy when it has direction, when it has beginning and purpose. If we have reflected on the ultimate meaning of events and relationships in our whole lives, then our own peace is contagious. Personal history can have a deeply spiritual dimension that children are very sensitive to. The values and attitudes that past experiences have engendered in us are evident to others. In the same way that genealogy gives a framework to sharing personal history, a healthy spirituality can give the story wings.

Richard remembers problems most clearly and shares them with an underlying sadness as if to say, "Life stinks! There have always been tragedies." On the other hand, Agnes shares most memories with a little smile, punctuating details with the phrase, "I'm so lucky. People have been good to me." The movie *Parenthood* featured a grandmother who thought of life as a roller coaster with lots of ups and downs. The thrill of the ride was worth it to her.

If we hope to bring our grandchildren to God, then it is time to see if God's word and actions have shaped us. It is helpful to look for ways in which Jesus has been a main character in the drama of our lives. If we believe that baptism immerses us into God's life, plunging every event and relationship into a divine plan of salvation, then it is only our awareness of God that is lacking. If this is difficult for us, we need other Christians to help us review our lives and the quality of our relationship with God. Perhaps we are being invited to a new level of faith.

As a college student I experienced a retreat that challenged me through "witnesses" by students willing to share what God had done through specific events in their lives. I was impressed! After my retreat I made an effort to think about daily events in the light of the Scriptures. I began reading one psalm a day so that there would be a dialogue between my life and God's word. Just a month later in the middle of a stormy night, our family's garage was struck by lightning and partially burned. It was a frightening experience for many reasons. For one thing, many of my grandparents' belongings were in storage on the second floor and were lost. I couldn't understand why God had allowed such a loss in their lives.

As I prayed on the porch steps afterward, I opened my Bible to Acts 3:1–10, the passage about the cure of a lame beggar. The beggar had asked Peter and John for alms. Peter replied, "I have neither silver nor gold, but I will give you what I have: in the name of Jesus Christ the Nazarene, walk!" As I reflected on the story I realized that it was to Peter's advantage that he didn't have pocket change or bread to give away. Perhaps it was to our advantage that we had fewer belongings because of the fire. My grandparents had been poor most of their lives, but they always opened their home to others, especially elderly relatives. Previous losses had given them compassion for others. God was inviting me to have the same outlook on life.

Scripture gives us many examples of an awareness of God's hand in large and small events of our life. For the Israelites, history was a celebration of what God had done. Events were like portraits of God's faithfulness rather than photographs stressing verifiable historic facts. Even their tragedies and sinfulness were seen in the light of God's covenant, God's everlasting love. For example, Psalms 78, 105, and 106 recount events in Israel's past as a nation. The Scripture writer reminds us that faith is built through remembering God's actions:

> Seek Yahweh and his strength,
> seek his face untiringly
> remember the marvels he has done,
> his wonders, the judgements from his mouth.
> — Psalm 105:4–5

God is at work in history. God acts in my history and in yours. All we need are the eyes to see God. Some of us may need guidance to deal with hurtful memories that are like juggernauts. If you do, I would recommend the book by the Linns listed in the bibliography. There are steps you can take. One personal example comes to mind. My dad was backing down a very steep hill that was covered with ice to get his three little girls home. With each skid we shrieked in terror from the back seat of the old black Studebaker. Our hearts and confidence were more frozen than the roadway. To see God's hand in this difficult memory, I would let myself relive it in the presence of Jesus. The imagination can be a wonderful tool for healing. I would picture Jesus in the back seat with us. He might have on a funny red circus hat and hand out roller coaster tickets. Then he would say, "Squeeze my hand. We'll scream and laugh together. I'll keep you safe." If you need guidance in praying through bad memories, there are steps you can take.

Guardian of Past and Future

When we have experienced God's actions in our lives there is still a need to be sensitive in the way we describe an event. Most people think of faith as an intimate subject, and with good reason. Jesus touches us very deeply. It is almost always appropriate to share our feelings about a past event. If we are asked why we felt that way, then perhaps we can go further. It is important not to moralize when we share faith stories, but leave our loved ones free to draw their own conclusions. For example, if we are sharing a story that recalls fear we can ask, "Were you ever scared too? What do you do if it happens?" A loved one's open-ended future is an important counterpoint to a grandparent's past.

As encouraging as words and stories can be, they are only part of being a family historian. The job description covers a lot more than sharing memories and stories. There are tasks that make us like curators for a family museum and guardians of both past and future at once. I'll never forget the thrill I experienced when Aunt Lillie handed me a little yellowed card that read, "An announcement of importance! The stork arrived the other day and we both kind of thought that you'd be interested now in hearing what he brought." It was my own birth announcement. Some of us have rooms or desks or diaries full of things we have saved. "Grandma's attic" is what we are talking about, even if it's only a cardboard box. As humans, we accumulate stuff that has emotional significance. Some of it becomes a living record of who we are and where we are going. Ninety-two percent of the grandparents that I surveyed often or always kept family records, momentos, or photos. These items are a real source of enjoyment for us. Aunt Lillie has a small collection of stories, photos, and letters in the side pouch on her automated chair. Nancy created a system of large Manila envelopes for each grandchild so that she can place objects in them from time to time. Jodie, who had polio in infancy, still mourns the fact that her family never took photos of her as a child, like they did of her sisters.

Sometimes the hard part of playing curator is knowing what to keep and what to throw out. Perhaps when you reach this point another question is helpful, "Am I guardian of the past for the sake of the future, or for its own sake?" We should save things that give grandchildren a foundation for the future. Glimpses of their early lives, family background, and rudimentary talents can give them the security to move forward. We do not want to give the impression that childhood was the best part of the story. Please don't stop adding to your treasures when a child reaches ten. On the other hand, trim down what you save, so that objects with the most meaning are kept.

As we play family historian, we develop insights into a grandchild's life story. Each of our young people has a personal biography in the making. It is exciting to watch it unfold as we make room in our hearts for yet another person's story. Monica is a lawyer. She describes herself as a future person. "I don't dwell in the past like so many of my friends. I might share something my mother did in caring for nine children, but I don't tell a lot of stories. I want to help Lisa prepare for the future." Monica does share items and insights from traveling. She makes an important point. We must support grandchildren as they journey forward, equipping them with a few small tools from the past.

One of the encouraging things for many grandparents is that a new child's story carries on family traditions and identity, giving new meaning to all that has gone before. All the generations become brothers and sisters in our hearts. If you have an interest in collecting photos, stories, and family records of your own ancestors as background for grandchildren, then you are embarking on a more sophisticated job as family historian. But don't get overwhelmed. Even if you do just a little bit to record memories of parents and grandparents, you will be assembling an irreplaceable family treasure. If you want to become a serious genealogist there are lots of resources to get you started at the local library. Others may not be interested just yet, but that isn't important. Be vocal about your efforts, so that anyone who is history-minded will hear about you. It may be a distant cousin's child, but your own definition of who is "family" will have broadened the more you get involved in genealogy.

As guardians of past and future we can also share one more perspective with our grandchildren. Just as we can provide clues to their beginning and biological roots, we can offer clues to their final destiny. Our own struggles with age, sickness, retirement, and death become a powerful example of their own frailty, old age, and death. Children do not think of these things as a common destiny but will be inspired or disheartened by the models they look back on in later years. This has happened to our daughter Rachel. She wrote:

> Six squished people traveled in a rusty Buick for seven lengthy hours. It was not one of our typical family trips to Massachusetts; it was anything but that. The silence in our car was louder than the noise of the tires on the rain-covered highway. It was appropriate weather for a funeral.

Friday night I had discovered that my grandmother had died. Disbelief shuddered through my body. Memere couldn't be dead. A week earlier I had spoken to her over the phone and she sounded perfectly healthy.

No one in my house slept particularly well that night. My mother, who was five month's pregnant, spent hours consoling my father. Sleep became burdensome for me. For the next few weeks nightmares and dreams and reality were all one cruel illusion. Memere's face was whiter and her red hair grayer, lying in the casket. Visions drifted in and out of the funeral parlor with prayerful lips, crying eyes, faces filled with grief. I sat or stood in a troubled daze trying to understand how life held purpose when there was death for someone I cared about.

A sense of grief remained with me for months afterward. I spent hours in search of hope. For the longest time I couldn't see the significance of her death in my life. Then one day soon after the birth of my little sister Katie, I noticed something. There was something familiar in Katie's face and her blue, blue eyes. It was the same expression I had often seen in my grandmother's eyes. Somehow Katie was a piece of my grandmother. A great sense of hope filled me after I discovered this wonderful continuation of spirit that dared to defy mortality.

We began this chapter with the Statue of Liberty and end it with a little baby's blue eyes (which are still the same bright navy blue almost two years later). Such is the nature of storytelling. I left out the one about Walter who was picking blueberries with his fiancée when a snake crawled up his pant leg. Each of us is a story animal. We could continue on and on with great variety and range of subject and emotion.

As grandparents we can share personal history through our stories. We can be living ancestors and family historians, searching out our own style of sharing memories, genealogy, spirituality, and events. We have status as official biographers for our grown children. Our vision of the uniqueness of each child and the wholeness of life from one generation to the next is the key. We can give grandchildren courage and direction through glimpses of their parent's childhood and their own treasured beginnings. Children are drawn to an adventure by inner magnetic force. It is up to us to see the events of our lives as colored by emotion, meaning, and faith. We can then give witness to the stories that we are. We don't have to be hit by lightning or take our shoes off in the snow. No matter what our past is like, each of us is novel and mystery, fiction and fact, fable and encyclopedia for our families.

≺ ○ ≻

For Reflection, Sharing, and Discussion

1. Each grandparent can be like a window on the family's past. We can be family historians, living ancestors, and official biographers for grown children. Which of these roles is most appealing? Which is least appealing? Why?

2. As we review our lives it is important to have a balanced appreciation for past, present, and future. Which do you find yourself focusing on most often? Which do you need God's help to let go of?

3. What part of your house is like a family museum or a "grandma's attic?" What could you do to make it more organized or accessible to your family in the future? What kinds of things do you like to save and why?

Activities

1. Ask a grandchild to help you tape-record a history of your life. (Many people find it artificial to talk to a machine alone.) Choose several topics, allowing five minutes per topic. Let the young person be the MC, introducing you and each topic. He or she might hold up cue cards: "One minute left." or "Time's up!" He or she might write com-

mercials for use in between topics. The same thing can be done in video.

- The story of my birth
- What I did as a child
- School back then was...
- How I met my spouse
- Our wedding day
- My saddest day was...
- I felt silly when...
- My job, my vocation
- A historical event...
- My parents...

2. A. Review major events in your life. Which was the clearest example of God's love and action in your life? Which one left you feeling furthest from God's care? Perhaps you would like to go back and imagine Jesus in that memory (see the Linns' book for help.)

B. Choose an event from your life to practice your history-sharing skills. Write the answers to these questions about the event to clarify your own thinking, not to offer an analysis of the event to family.

- What was the beginning of this one episode?
- How did I feel? How did others feel?
- What were the issues or conflicts?
- What is a good ending for sharing this story?

3. Try recording what you know about significant members of your family on a "Biography Bones" chart like

the one below. Each of us retains some mixture of facts and story snippets that make for good biography. Put only verifiable facts in the FACTS column. If you lean toward biography, collect story snippets from other family members. If you are interested in recording data, refer to books by Beller and Hilton in the bibliography.

PERSON	FACTS	STORY SNIPPETS
Walter	lived 1897–1972	snake episode while blueberrying
Young	married 1920	raised by mom and grandparents
	constable 1931–35	met wife at local swimming pond

4. Develop a family tree. Begin with grandchildren, listing dates and places of birth. On a second line list your grown children and their spouses with birth information. List the dates and places of marriage also. On a new line list yourself and also your spouse, giving the same data for each of you. A fourth line names your parents' generation, giving dates for births, marriages, and deaths. If you are unsure of your information, add a large question mark next to an uncertain entry.

Some grandparents like to fill out keepsake albums that include family trees, like *Grandmother Remembers* produced by Carlton Cards (Box 660270, Dallas, TX 75266). Others like to use more precise charts like those recommended in books by Beller or Hilton in the bibliography. Charts can also be purchased at the nearest Mormon church.

CHAPTER 5

Natural Paths to Father-God

---

*L*ET ME INTRODUCE TWO GRANDMOTHERS, Florence and Virginia. Both would like to share more of God's love with their families. Both sing hymns as lullabies to their small grandchildren.

It had been a long day for Florence. She was babysitting for little Melissa. There were still toys to put away and dishes to do. Florence was spent in more ways than her tired body could enumerate. Bedtime was a special treat though, a time for snuggling. She enjoyed singing to the little toddler. Melissa's eyes would grow round with wonder and delight as Florence whispered little tunes about Jesus. Then they would scurry into the baby's room and sing again, looking at a picture of Jesus and some children. Melissa liked to pretend she was in the picture that Nana gave her. It was fun to decide what Jesus was doing with his little friends. Tonight it was hide and seek, probably because Mommy and Daddy were gone.

When I talked to Florence a few days later, she had a lot of feelings to share. She was dissatisfied with attempts to share faith with her grandchildren. Melissa's bedtime ritual wasn't enough, according to Florence. When I congratulated her on the music and imaginary story time, she replied, "But I'm the only one that does that! I wish they'd go to church more often." Florence is worried and frustrated, like many grandparents.

Virginia chuckled as she, too, described her use of religious songs with eighteen grandchildren, especially when they were little. "I had to change my tune at one point," she confessed. I used to sing, "His Name Is Wonderful," a song that describes Jesus as Lord. Then one Christmas Brian burst into tears when we put the baby Jesus in the manger. He marched over and told us to fix Jesus. We didn't know what he meant. We added a little blanket. That was no good. We fastened the baby into Mary's arms with a rubber band and still he cried. Finally we asked Brian to straighten out the problem. He threw the plastic baby in the rubbish and put one of the wise men in the tiny manger exclaiming, "His name is wonderful! He's the King!"

So many of us hope to bring our grandchildren and families to God. That desire is in itself a gift, and we are blessed when we can enjoy these stirrings as gift. Perhaps only a few of us are like Virginia and can chuckle at our own attempts to share faith. Too many of us are more like Florence. We see only what is lacking and succumb to worry.

It may be helpful to step back from the situation. Let's imagine ourselves as walking in the woods with our families. We have come to a small clearing surrounded by huge oak trees, a few beech, and a stand of young white birch off to one side. We have our choice of several paths: one narrow, older, twisting path, and another wide lane created by a ranger's jeep. A third path is freshly hewn, with broken branches on either side and a rut created by a large tree trunk that had been hauled out of the area. We know that one of these paths will lead us to safety, food, and shelter. Perhaps our grown children have already chosen a path and we suspect it's the wrong one. Perhaps they are almost out of ear-shot and we feel compelled to do something. We know that one path leads to Jesus. "Which one?" we ask with the psalmist.

> Yahweh, make your ways known to me,
> teach me your paths.
> Set me in the way of your truth, and teach me,
> for you are the God who saves me.
> — Psalm 25:4–5

Our faith in Jesus helps us imagine him standing right beside us in the woods. I see him with long, flowing robes, like a priest at Mass. Perhaps we would cry out to Jesus from the wooded clearing, like the mother in Matthew's Gospel.

> Then the mother of Zebedee's sons came with her sons to make a request of him, and bowed low; and he said to her, "What is it you want?" She said to him, "Promise that these two sons of mine may sit one at your right hand and the other at your left in your kingdom."
>
> — Matthew 20:20–22

This mother needed details and assurances. So do we. Let's call out to him also. He is the Way, the Truth, and the Life. Jesus is himself the road and the path to our Father-God. We want all that for our families too. "Which path up ahead? The twisted narrow one, the jeep's lane, or the freshly cut road?" we would ask. We need to know.

Look for Vegetation and Signs

The desire to bring our children and grandchildren to God can be like a compass for us. We can take steps to follow that desire. It is a call to seek our own ongoing conversion, then to become evangelists, which simply means "bringing the good news into all strata of humanity, and through its influence transforming humanity from within and making it new."[10] In the gospel story, Jesus responded to the mother's desire by asking her two sons if they would follow him. We too can be part of God's invitation. If our methods are shaped by the reality of God's love, then our grandchildren will be evangelized. How they respond to God's love is up to them. They must stand in their own clearing and choose a path. It is our privilege to be a part of the revelation of God's love so that grandchildren will have a real choice.

It is interesting that the church requires an extra set of "parents" when a baby is baptized and commitments are first voiced. In a certain sense, this is illogical. The parents will be primary religious educators for their children. Still, the church recognizes the power of family and community to engender faith. Children absorb God's love like thirsty plants in a wood or garden. If we are a significant part of their lives they can drink in God's loving presence as a part of their relationships with us. Our desires for them are a reflection of that truth also.

Mary brought her grandson Michael and his cousin Leo to the arcade so they could play a few video games. On her way back to Michael's house she happened to pass the cemetery and decided to stop and visit her parents' grave. She and the boys got out for a moment. Leo was very curious. He had never been to a cemetery before, even though he was twelve. She lengthened her expedition and showed Leo where his grandparents, great-grandparents, and even their parents were buried. He wanted paper and pencil to write their names down. By now, Michael was back in the car playing with a new key chain alarm. Mary asked Leo how he felt about being there.

"What do you mean," he asked.

"Well, some people don't like cemeteries," Mary said. "They get scared or worried about dying."

"Oh, no!" declared Leo, "This is a nice quiet place. I thought when somebody died, they just got shoved in a bag and put out with the trash. This is nice."

Grandparents can be like part-time gardeners, watching for ways in which God is already acting and alive in their families. Our faith should help us celebrate what God is doing, then wait patiently for "teachable moments" to address what is lacking.

Gloria was very upset that her children do not attend church services. I asked her what good things were going on in their lives that she could thank God for. Gloria answered, "Nothing. If they don't watch out, they'll all go to hell!" She may be very aware of the primary choice they face. Her heart, however, is so full of fear and condemnation that she has become blind to God's incredible mercy for her own children. Unfortunately, that kind of blindness can be contagious. It would be very difficult for her family to be reconciled to God through Gloria. God does not withdraw love, not even in response to serious sin.

When we have a clear vision of what is possible, we will notice signs and teachable moments. These are special times of awareness and questioning. Leo wanted to know more and Mary was wise enough to notice. Some children have questions that will lead them on a search for God. Other children respond to nature and can find the Creator behind animals and birds. Still others are most at home with groups of people and will recognize God in a communal setting.

In the 1970s an official document was prepared to define the fundamental vision of Roman Catholic religious education in our country. It tells us what we can watch for too. This text, *Sharing the Light of Faith, National Directory for Catholics of the United States*, describes the movements of God's revelation and personal concern in terms of signs. There are concrete realities we can help our families experience. "The signs of God's saving activity have come to be classified under four general headings: biblical signs, liturgical signs, ecclesial signs, and natural signs."[11] The document also urges us to strive for a harmony between all these realities. We must hope that our whole lives will come together in the person of Jesus Christ.

As we become more aware of how these signs apply to our families, we will grow in hope. There is a lot we can do to foster religious experience, no matter what is happening in a grandchild's family. Each of us is called to be an evangelist and catechist by virtue of our faith in Jesus. We may need help to understand what evangelization means in this most important relationship. It means many things and is acted out in a variety of ways by different believers. As grandparents, we have an advantage in sharing religious tradition and faith.

Simply because [we] are present to the child, we are signs of the tradition and transcendent.... There is something special in the whole context of being a generation beyond one's parents' generation.... Tradition stretches back before their parents began to live and touches the "unknown."...This touches their identity and tells the child concretely about his or her own story. It communicates the values of life and reason for existence.[12]

Gifts of Awe and Wonder

All physical life is a *natural* sign of God's love and activity. There is a real miracle involved in the way babies and children grow. Babies begin as explosions of tiny living particles invisible to the naked eye. Children experience explosions of activity, language, and learning. The field of religious education points out the importance of human growth as a foundation for faith. Children grow into religious faith only after experiencing a healthy "natural" faith. In other words, after they learn to trust mothers, chairs, refrigerators, teachers, and computers, then they can learn to trust God.

If we respect nature as a path to God and religious faith, then we must redefine what brings children to God. Things like tying shoes and buying cookies must take on a new significance. These activities are as important as formal religious training or memorizing doctrine and creeds. We must value human growth. The excitement of childhood advances and milestones, like learning to smile or wave "bye-bye" are precious gifts. Such gifts will be used to relate to family, world, and God. Our humanity is an important context for a life of faith.

Grandparents often experience a sense of life as gift. This puts us on the cutting edge of a vivid faith in Father-God as creator of all life. Jill talks to babies and toddlers about how beautiful they are. She holds up a foot and says, "Thank you, God, for these toes." She touches a belly and says,

"Thank you, Father, for this little tummy and the food inside." She prays the connection that grandparents are keenly aware of.

We can help grandchildren appreciate nature too. We can share gifts of awe and wonder at the universe. We can look at leaves twice. We can stop our cars to admire a cherry tree. We can cradle a broken toy or invite a youngster to pick up litter on a sidewalk. Little children are naturally filled with wonder. A two-year-old doesn't walk to a destination, but explores every item along the way as a destination of its own. We can be two years old in our outlook on the world, drawing grandchildren into an awareness of God as creator.

For those who are oriented by five very physical senses, experiencing nature as a sign of God's love is a simple task. They can simply admire God's handiwork out loud, for a child's sake. Others may be more at home with thought and intuition than with five senses. For them, the natural sensuality of a child can be disorienting. These grandparents might share an understanding of nature with our grandchildren as they get older. Art's favorite part of grandparenting is talking about "how things work and why they exist." He likes to analyze clouds and bushes and motorcycles with his youngsters.

We can help children realize that God is artist, craftsman, and scientist. God has the eyes of a Rembrandt, the insights of an architect, and the mind of an Einstein. We can share any of these stances toward the world with our grandchildren. We can help children look carefully at the world, and then again at the producer of it all. My grandfather took me fishing a few times. When we caught fish he took the time to show me scales, fins, and gills, then explain how they worked. Of course, I suspect he had his limits in dealing with all the scientific curiosity he had aroused. After a generous amount of questions were answered he would say, "Shh! We have to be quiet or we'll scare the fish away."

God is an artist who gives substance to the divine personality in the nature of trees and fish and constellations.

St. Therese of Lisieux referred to God that way in her auto-biography. There is a tremendous power in God's creativity that makes a major earthquake look like a ripple in a puddle. God is also an inventor who is keenly aware of the properties and limits of God's inventions. We need to call on this merciful inventor in order to develop sensitivity to his creation.

Our grandchildren need more than a romantic notion of Father-God as a botanist in a rose garden. Future generations must let God "father" the whole universe in their imaginations in order to deal with overwhelming issues like technology, environmental pollution, and nuclear power. We can invite young people on a mission to restore and recreate God's handiwork.

It is a task that requires a very large faith. Where will they find such faith, if not in Jesus? Where will they hear of him, if we choose to be silent?

God-Genes in Our Family

When we talk about our understanding and attitudes toward nature, we come in contact with the more specific reality of *human nature*. Our view of the human person is a key factor in evangelizing our families. It can be a sign of God's Reign, or a hindrance along the path to Christian faith. It shapes many other values and decisions that families face. We may find ourselves at odds over questions like, "Should families try to eat supper together every night?" or "When does family life take precedence over individual commitments?" Our answers are a reflection of our understanding of human nature.

For some of us, it is one of life's painful mysteries that we do not share important values with our children and grand-children. "What is this world coming to?" we ask. Boldly, we proclaim, "This isn't the way I raised them!" We would like to believe that "God-genes" are passed from one generation to the next, like genes for blue eyes or large bone structure, and that respect, compassion, and holiness can be passed around like Christmas presents.

Indeed, being a parent allows us an insider's view of God's dilemma in the Garden of Eden. Eternal happiness was laid out for the taking, but something went wrong, something we call "original sin" that affects us all. This happened at the dawn of human life, but still has its effects now. Something has kept going wrong with every page of human life since then. Our Father did not guarantee or engineer automatic holiness through "God-genes." What God did leave us, to cope with sin, is his own nature, reflected in our humanity. We are made of "God stuff"! We are built in the image of God. We are also given Jesus, *the* Son of God to help us overcome sin.

We must see each family member as fashioned by God, having inherent dignity and worth. Each loved one is re-deemed by Jesus and can be reorientated toward God's life. Each of us is also empowered by the Holy Spirit to choose rightly. God's Reign can be "what this world is coming to," what we are headed for. We can rely on these truths.

Most of us experience a life-long struggle in holding on to such a vision without being distracted by sin and emotional blindness. A quick look at our past can be an opportunity to grow in compassion for others. Our own actions, values, and priorities may have been in line with the Gospel, neutral, or even contrary to our faith. We must have the courage to look, so that we can clarify ourselves as signs of God's revelation. We do not want to be hindrances along the path.

At the time of their marriage, Billie and Fran were three month's pregnant. They experienced only a mediocre rela-tionship over the next seventeen years. It was a blessing for them to experience a Marriage Encounter. A lot of healing and affirmation took place. But just a few months later their teenage daughter announced her own unwed pregnancy. They were crushed and felt so helpless. "We did the best we could," Fran told me. "But all she saw was our weak-nesses. I don't know what will happen to Debby, but I know what we have decided. The brokenness stops now. We are going to work at our faith and be whole, no matter what it takes."

The values and actions that our grown children and grandchildren espouse will often challenge us and act as catalyst for personal, inner examinations. This is good. We want a faith that is relevant and alive. But this is not easy, nor is it good to stop here. We can also look at their lives in order to affirm values that are in line with the Gospel message. Remember, they are made in God's image. God's Spirit is at work in their hearts. The picture of the human person in their hearts may be incomplete, or inconsistent, but God is at work shaping their vision.

Jean was befuddled by her son-in-law's decision to skip a mortgage payment and drive his family to Disneyland for a vacation. They would stay with nearby relatives and get by on peanut butter sandwiches. It would be their first real vacation away since the couple married three years earlier, the second marriage for each of them. In Jean's way of thinking this was fiscal irresponsibility, but she stopped and thought for a while. Instead of condemning them, she was able to send them off and say, "I don't understand what you're doing, but I'm proud of the way you work at building new family memories together."

When we notice values and actions that are not in line with our faith, it is difficult to resist the urge to straighten things out. Sometimes we can't help ourselves. At these times, we may want to concentrate on providing "active listening." We can listen for desires, then report them to family members. In the example above, we might say, "You want to show your children how much you love them." Such listening can help young people sort through their own values and choices. Rules cannot be loaned or given as gifts. They are only borrowed values. Ultimately, a toddler abandons eating with fingers in order to imitate the rest of the family, not just on a parent's say-so.

God Read Us an Important Story

Additional signs of God's revelation focus less on physical and human nature and more on God's direct actions. One of these is Scripture, a *biblical* sign of God's love. To some of us, reading Scripture is as foreign as finding a library shelf on a secluded path. At first glance we see a book filled only with nouns, verbs, and fairy tales. But it is what we see at second glance with the eyes of faith that is important. Which glance do you turn toward this story? Which glance does your family use? Is it the same? How can you come to cherish God's Word together?

This would be a good time to introduce you to one of my spiritual grandparents who was not a blood relative. Ed Dolan was a boarder in my family's home for several years. He was a retired high school teacher, looking for a way to continue his work with young people. I was a confused teenager, and I was more confused by his intrusion into my life and family.

I remember avoiding Mr. Dolan as best I could, until one angry confrontation after school in the kitchen. He asked about my day, and I told him that I hated him. It was that simple in my mind, but not in his. Ed turned to me and asked, "Do you really?" Then he left me to my own devices. His love and acceptance won me over. We became good friends. I could talk to him about all sorts of things: college plans, boy friends, novels, and world peace. He wasn't afraid of any topic, not even the ones my parents were reluctant to consider.

Then Ed Dolan fell and broke his hip on the way to teach a religion class. He was discouraged and depressed about this new limitation. A priest suggested that he read the Bible as he convalesced. So he dusted off our copy with the red print for words that Jesus spoke, and he began to experience the power of God's Spirit. I was intrigued. There were times when I knocked on his door and he was in another world. I sensed a deeper joy and peace about him than I had ever experienced before. It was almost embarrassing to look in his eyes.

After that I wanted to really read the Bible, not just look at the pages, nodding my head to familiar stories. I wanted the kind of reading that starts with the heart and soul, then the eyes. Mr. Dolan's experience was contagious and dynamic.

> Yes, as the rain and the snow come down from the heavens and do not return without watering the earth, making it yield and giving growth to provide seed for the sower and bread for the eating, so the word that goes from my mouth does not return to me empty, without carrying out my will and succeeding in what it was sent to do.
>
> — Isaiah 55:10–11

God's Word in Scripture is addressed to your family too. To grow in this awareness, you may want to read *Reading Scripture as the Word of God* by George Martin (Ann Arbor, Mich.: Word of Life, 1975). God's Word is a living word for us, and our loved ones, spoken in power. Sometimes we can only wait for that power to "take," the way we wait for penicillin to kick in when a child has an ear infection.

In the meanwhile, we can present Scripture to grand-children alongside other parts of our shared life. If we read stories together, we can include Bible stories in our repertoire. Arch Books produced by Concordia are a good choice for children. Remember to make the characters in the story real by adding your own voice and personality to the Scripture event. We might consider reading a short piece of Scripture at meal time, especially if we are willing to share what touches us about it without preaching.

The biblical signs of God's love are as numerous as the images and symbols that probe and describe our most inner realities. What we do with these signs is limited only by our degree of willingness to let Scripture touch us on a daily basis. If these symbols are a vital part of our thinking, then they will spill out. A tired spouse will look like the apostles coming in from a fishing trip. An ornery grandchild will seem like the feisty friends who dropped the crippled man in through the roof to get help from Jesus.

One of the challenges of Scripture is its connectedness to daily life and to the church that produced it. If we found a book on a secluded path in the woods, we would wonder where it came from. In the same way, we must have a respect for the Bible's origins, keeping an eye out for interdependence of ecclesial and liturgical signs of God's love. When we try to separate Scripture from its moorings, we run the risk of misinterpretation and a watered down ability to heal and bless our families.

The Church Gathers in the Woods

Each of us has experienced God in a variety of ways throughout our lives. All these events give us a personal spirituality, a style of relating to God. For most of us this has happened in the context of church or parish life. We want this same life for our families. We want them to know Jesus through sacraments like Eucharist, baptism, and marriage. (These are *liturgical* signs of God's love.) We also want more than warm bodies in cold pews. We realize the importance of really belonging to a community of believers, following moral teaching, and being swept up in worship. This is the *ecclesial* sign of God's love. Somehow we sense that a Christian life is shallow without it. We have experienced a gathering in the woods that inspired us to continue, and like the Gospel writers, we realize an invitation to follow Jesus includes a network of relationships with disciples and apostles.

Hopefully, our own involvement in church life has given our children and grandchildren a sense of being invited into a faith community. After all, they were right beside us in the pew. But were they? For our generation the pew was a lot longer than it is now. There was often a network of believing adults in neighborhood, families, and even ethnic groupings that was church for us. Now the ecclesial sign is often weakened. Church is not all around us. The pew is shorter.

This does not mean that Jesus has stopped offering his church and sacraments to our families. It does not mean that we should give up in our hopes for unity with them. The Spirit of God still reaches out in power. What it does mean is more understanding and compassion for the religious experience of younger generations. It means learning how the church builds community today so that we can be more effective. For some grandparents it may mean learning about other denominations that family members are involved in.

Bert Ghezzi, editor of *Keeping Your Kids Catholic*, describes a study of young people who have decided not to belong to the Catholic Church. As many as 42 percent of all Catholics leave the church at some time in their lives. In the study cited, three categories of dropouts emerge:

> More than half of young dropouts are in the family-tension category. These young persons experience pressure or problems in their family, and at the first chance rebel against their parents and the church.
>
> Weary or "bored" dropouts (about one-fourth) are persons who no longer have any motivation for attending church. . . . They usually give some recent external event as a reason for leaving but . . . "An inner faith and spiritual life is lacking, hence motivation is weak."
>
> Another large group of Catholics (about 20 percent) leave the church because their lifestyle conflicts with church teaching. Usually their difficulty stems from moral problems.[13]

These reasons challenge us to a wide range of responses as grandparents and parents. First, it is important to look at the quality of our relationships with our young people so that religious issues do not become a symptom or "smoke screen" for other problems. Then it is good to be sensitive to the moral choices that are a part of choosing a religious community and responding to ecclesial and liturgical signs of God's love.

One poor grandmother had encouraged her daughter to get an abortion, thinking that it would be a solution for all concerned. When this daughter married the following year she was quickly reconciled to the church, but over the next five years she and her family were adrift, moving from Baptist, to Episcopalian, to Presbyterian congregations. The grandmother was disappointed, but realized there was pain and spiritual confusion involved. She had even contributed to the problem.

Our own faithfulness to sacraments can be an invitation into the Body of Jesus. We can make our families feel welcome by treating sacraments as special occasions in our grandchildren's lives. These are moments when we can make an effort to spend a little time alone with them, perhaps sharing expectations, feelings, and a family religious treasure. Our confidence in God's love through sacraments will speak to them.

We can also foster experiences with the ecclesial signs of God's love in our grandchildren's lives. I'll let Michael tell you how his grandmother did this. We will explore additional ideas in the next chapter.

Dear Grandma,

When my Mom makes me a grilled cheese sandwich, I always remember how much better yours tasted. I'll always remember how I enjoyed the M & Ms you brought home for me every day, and the times you took care of me when my Mom was at school. When I was a little boy, you wiped away my tears. When I fell and skinned my knee, you made me feel better. I'll always remember the day you taught me the sign of the cross. I feel sorry that you missed my First Communion, but I know that even if you're in heaven, you will always be with me.

Love,
Your grandson, Michael (Hayes)

Penny is another example. Her daughter married a minister in a fundamentalist church. She respected the zeal of their faith and even attended her grandchildren's baptisms. Her son-in-law, Doug, would try to convince her about the merits of his own congregation from time to time. Once, when he shared a Scripture passage with her, she thanked him and replied, "Doug, you know so much about the Bible. It's too bad you don't know more about the church. Did you ever wonder how much more you could do for God if you loved his church?" Penny's comment intrigued Doug. He began to attend Catholic conferences and prayer meetings. He and his family, and part of his congregation, were eventually converted back to Catholicism.

God Reaches Out to My Family

Sometimes, it is not a question of what we can *do* to help our families experience the church. Sometimes God must reach out to them in his own way. Abraham and Mary are models of letting God do the unexpected. Abraham wanted sons and grandsons. He was full of plans and ideas, but God did not act according to plan. Abraham had to learn to cherish his wife and son, so that the intimacy itself was God's plan. At the time of Jesus, heaven was described as being "in the bosom of Abraham" (Luke 16:22), a very grandfatherly image. Mary surrendered the desire to have children, and perhaps even grandchildren, to God. The Father rewarded such a sacrifice. God gave her all people in history as her own children.

We are not alone in the desire to draw our children into the church. It is the mission of the whole body. Sometimes we must surrender the idea of being primary channels and be aware of opportunities the church offers. There are programs for teens, whole families, and individuals who are searching. It may be appropriate to invite a grandchild or even a child's whole family to attend one of these programs with you.

In our diocese we have workshops to help families celebrate Christmas and Easter together. It is not uncommon for a grandparent to bring family members for an afternoon of prayer, music, discussion, and crafts. One mother told us,

"The girls held onto the nativity figures they made, and even brought them to bed. These little bits of paper were so precious to them.... They gained a rich memory of the meaning of Christmas.... For a little while we put aside the stress of family life and concentrated on our love for God." Perhaps grandparents could ask for more family religious education programs and use such programming as invitations to deeper faith. You might ask your parish director of religious education about possibilities, offering suggestions and perhaps personal involvement.

There are also adult education opportunities, parish and regional prayer groups, and a program called the Rite of Christian Initiation for Adults who want full membership in the church. You may want to invite family members to one of these outreach efforts. It would be ideal if your extended family could be your religious community as well. When this is not possible, we must take responsibility for our need to belong to a faith-sharing community. Then we will draw renewed strength and be more capable of bringing family to Jesus.

We must think of our efforts at evangelization as introducing loved ones to a dear friend, Jesus, not as mandates for a certain kind of behavior. We must die to our own precious rules about how God does things in our family. We are called as church to embrace the brokenness of those in our midst, in our families, gently lifting them up for our Father-God to kiss.

God is not stingy with his love. There are signs of it all around us. There are signs of it in our grandchildren's lives. There are the movements of nature that reflect God's nature, the complexity of a thousand prisms in a bee's eye, the tumult of a waterfall, the rich smell of soil. There is the message and sign of the human person, "fearfully and wonderfully" made, each of us with dignity and giftedness.

There are the Scriptures, "our Big Book full of stories of our people who have also journeyed from slavery to freedom and through death to life."[14] There is the church, broken but blessed as we trudge along the path in the woods, saints and angels all around us pointing the way back home.

≺ ο ≻

For Reflection, Sharing and Discussion

1. God is revealed to us through nature, Scripture, and church. Which of these is the clearest sign of God's love for you? Which is the most difficult? Why?

2. How has your attitude about human nature been shaped by God's revelation in the person of Jesus? What difficulties do you have in understanding the human condition?

3. How has the Bible been a living word from God in your life? What is it about Scripture that you might like to share with members of your family?

4. What was your experience of bringing your own children to church when they were growing up? How do you share membership in the Body of Jesus with them now?

Activities

1. Try a treasure hunt in the park or woods with a grandchild. Look for things you both like. After you are done exploring, write a thank-you note to God or a litany. Perhaps you might even seal your letter and drop it off at church.

2. Bring a grandchild to a church. Ask permission if necessary. Time alone in the building allows the youngster to explore, touch, and ask questions. Help your grandchild look for vital religious symbols and share what they mean to you. Be sure to leave time for prayer. Silent prayer together is okay after the age of seven. For younger children it is better to pray aloud with them.

3. Choose a grown child or grandchild, then take a few moments to think about what signs of God's love are strongest in his or her life. Spend time thanking God for what you see. Think about what signs are weakest. Tell God how you feel about this and ask God's help.

CHAPTER 6

Choose Life-giving Activities

---

*L*UCY IS GOOD at helping her family recycle clothing that grandchildren have outgrown. She can size up toddler or teen within seconds, and then compute what clothing would be best. When she arrived at my house with a bag full of items for Mary and Katie, I laughed. The T-shirt she was wearing caught my eye: "If I knew grandchildren would be so much fun, I would have had them first!"

There is a hustle-bustle kind of joy that comes from sharing life with our families. The particular style and activities we adopt may vary quite a bit. After all, grandparenting is usually only a part-time occupation for most of us. Diversity of talents, complexity of relationships, and geographic location all affect how we spend time with grandchildren. The dynamics of grandparenting also differ for men and women. But perhaps one of the greatest hazards of our world is concentrating on our differences, to the point that we lose confidence in our unity of heart and purpose.

As spiritual grandparents we share a vision of the fullness of life for our loved ones so we can adopt spiritual growth principles as criteria for the activities we choose together. This means we hope to share learning, service, prayer, and community with them for the sake of a well-rounded Christian life. It also means fostering a grandchild's talents with an eye toward their future development. We can draw them into an appreciation for visual, literary, and performing arts as a way of sharpening their awareness of life. We want to choose activities of long-lasting value. It is the nature of love, especially God's love, that we hope to experience together. God's incarnate involvement with us can be our model.

> The Word was made flesh,
> he lived among us,
> and we saw his glory,
> the glory that is his as the only son of the Father,
> full of grace and truth.
>
> —John 1:14

Mary's two grandmothers offer a striking example of the different ways that love can take flesh. Agnes has a passion for cooking and interior decorating. Mary enjoys the activity and learning at her house. Mary's other grandmother, Evelyn, is confined to a wheelchair, but she is a storyteller and a listener. Mary can share secrets and past adventures with her. Both are treasured people in her life. Both are present to her in love. It is the sharing of time and persons that flavors both relationships. Both have found very different activities to help them maintain ties with Mary.

It is good that each grandparent is unique. A child with grandparents who are willing to share themselves and their unique talents is very fortunate indeed. We need not compete with each other. The giving of self in families can flourish with careful respect for different definitions of visiting, babysitting, and just plain fun. A grandparent's life affords room for all kinds of activities, if we first make room for grandchildren in our hearts and accept ourselves for what we can offer.

Appointments Are a Family Matter

It is a challenge to offer ourselves in ways that can be appreciated and meet real needs. It is also hard work to take our cues from a grandchild's interests, especially when they are young or live far away or are unaccustomed to intimate relationships with adults. There will also be work involved for grandparents who want to choose life-giving activities versus just entertainment. Also, finding a common time or making a date with a grandchild can be the greatest challenge. We may need the courage to ask for specific agreements about how often we spend time together and what kinds of activities we hope to share.

There was a time in the early years of our marriage when John and I struggled with the need to balance his busy schedule, the care of three preschool children, and our commitment to spend time alone together. The situation was frustrating at best, volatile at worst. I actually bought myself a weekly schedule book, called John's office, and made an appointment to go to a movie. As I was pencilling in the date, I realized that my week's activities were very disorganized. Since then, we have learned to schedule together once a week and support each other in setting priorities to our commitments. We also schedule with our children at the beginnings of vacations and school semesters. It is a concrete way for us to value our relationships and work out expectations together. We try to do the same thing when visiting relatives for an extended amount of time. It was awkward at first, but now most people appreciate the clarity that scheduling adds.

Agreements, appointments, and dates are a way of life in our society. Teens juggle school, part-time jobs, and social activities. Children, and even preschoolers, are affected. Just last month we had a tenth birthday party for Tim. There was a need to extend the festivities by an hour after the invitations went out. Notifying parents was a very revealing experience. Most had to make major shifts in their itineraries. One child had to cancel. Another came for half the party. There was social bedlam.

Grandparents may be creating even more confusion by suggesting leisurely activities at a moment's notice. It's better to embrace the insanity of scheduling together. The management of activities is a way of making choices about who we are becoming. Some families need to rethink the priorities they have placed on their time; but we are not in a position to complain if we don't work at organizing our own lives. Such an attempt will give us compassion and insights into our own priorities.

If you have tried to make dates to share activities with family members, you may have noticed that difficulties arise. The more sporadic and weaker relationships can't always sustain so much honesty. It takes courage and self-awareness to tell others what you want and to give them the freedom to do the same. Some people find it helpful to separate the process into steps. Step one is listing everything both people would like. Each person generates at least three possibilities, either verbally or on paper. Step two involves evaluating possibilities together. Step three is the decision.

Once my daughter Mary and I were trying to decide on a way to spend a Saturday together. I listed a trip to the beach, playing Scrabble, and the library. Mary listed the video arcade, walking, and shopping in the mall. We didn't share a lot of interests. Next we looked at all six items and said what each of us liked *and* disliked about all six. It was hard work to see good points about each other's choices. It was important for me to discover that there was something I liked about malls. Since I enjoy sending greeting cards, going to the mall would give me more time to browse through cards than I usually allow myself. We had more in common than I thought at first glance.

What Do You Want to Do?

In the cartoon movie called *The Jungle Book* a boy travels through a desolate area and comes across vultures perched in a dead tree. The black creatures are frozen in unending dialogue. One asks, "What do you want to do?" Another responds, "I dunno, what do you want to do?" Still another adds, "I dunno, what do you want to do?" And so they remain, perched on the edge of relating to one another, isolated in their own inertia.

When we have the courage to tell each other what we

want there can be new clarity of purpose. We can untangle our expectations. We may need to discuss issues like the length of our visit, the expectations of one grandchild over another, and the ages of the children. Claire can visit only for a day on a monthly basis. She likes to spend time with everyone, but also enjoys being alone with each of her four grandchildren. Claire's family decided that each child would get an hour with Nana, but she would take only one child per visit. The others know that their turn is either one, two, or three months away. Susan has three grandchildren, but spends time alone only with the children who are over four years old. As she explained it, "There is more of them to love, and I don't have the strength to chase a toddler any more." She settles for reading story books to the little ones.

In order to make plans together, we must face our gifts and limits as human persons. Somehow we want to orchestrate both elements so that we can enjoy each other in God's presence. Sheila hires a babysitter to help her when her grandchildren come for a visit. Edna must ask her grandchildren not to play radios or televisions in the living room so that she doesn't get a headache from her hearing aid.

The exciting thing is that each of us is gifted. We can give a respectful nod to limits and then concentrate on talents we have received from a loving Father. These bits of personality, interest, and ability can be the guiding principles behind the activities we choose. Imogene noticed that her seven-year-old granddaughter is very inquisitive, especially about nature. Her response was to take Julie Ann on a trip to Howe Caverns. Her grandson Billy is more physically active and interested in animals. Imogene and Billy visited a petting zoo. She thoroughly enjoyed both outings and the way the children came to life doing things that fostered their interests. Bonny is a long-distance gramma. She gave Brian a folder for Christmas and sends him newspaper and magazine clippings about animals. Sometimes she asks Brian to send a story or drawing in response to the clipping.

Talents Lead the Way

We may also begin with a gift or talent of our own that we would like to share with grandchildren. This is wise only if we have a healthy relationship or if we have noticed an interest on their part. Young people need time to fall in love with something new or foreign and to experience it on their level first. We can help by breaking activities down into manageable pieces and talking about the physical sensations involved. Grandpa gave Freddie his own fenced-off area in the yard for planting radishes. Grandma gave Ellen her own length of cloth to make a doll blanket.

> I watch my grandma in autumn
> with the sun golden as a flaming bush
> lighting up the garden.
>
> She wares her green pants and orange hat
> like a marigold or chrysanthemum.
> She walks through rows
> where corn stands at attention
> or melon vines spread their fingers on the ground.
>
> She waves to me and I put this memory in my special book.
> The image of my grandmother on an ordinary day
> that turned to gold!
>
> — Katie Cooper

There are also primary human gifts that we can share with grandchildren. Our experiences with the arts underline vital elements of our humanity. Visual arts celebrate what we can see, touch, and make with our hands. Literary arts plunge us into the power of language. Performing arts highlight our human doings. The enjoyment and creation of all these can stimulate and console us. Scientists are learning that we actually have two very different parts to our brains that need activity and involvement. The "left brain" manages math, logic, analysis, perception of order, and speech. The "right brain" manages intuition, recognition of symbols, music, and emotions. Each of us benefits by the interchange between the two that visual, literary, and performing arts demand.

Music is perhaps the most widely accepted art form. Even small babies respond to melodies, and toddlers enjoy playing with both words and tunes. I like to chant with children between the ages of one and five, making up story songs as I go. This is a handy way to relate to a little one on the phone. Once a two-year-old boy named Mike spotted my husband's guitar on the floor during a workshop we were teaching. He edged his way over to touch it. I showed him how to pat the strings like a kitty. When I started humming a tune, though it was only loosely related to his strumming, his eyes lit up with wonder. He started humming too! Next, I chanted a story using his name. It was a pitiful tune, musically speaking, but that wasn't important. It went something like this:

> Mike saw a guitar,
> and Mike touched the guitar,
> and it sang for him,
> and Mike was happy,
> and the guitar was happy.
> Mike touched his toes
> and Mike's toes were dancing too.
> Mike said good-bye to the guitar,
> and that was sad.
> Good-bye, happy guitar.

(Notice how often I sang his name.)

Once I was waiting for a plane in the Islip airport. Next to me was a grandmother and a one-year-old. She consoled the tired child with a chant, "Ah, Ah, Baby . . . Ah, Ah, Baby." I was riveted to my seat. It was the same chant my mother-in-law used with babies. I have since wished that I had asked the woman if her family was from Scotland, like Mum's.

Chanting, dancing, storytelling, and even making mud pies are some of the first steps we take as human artists. Grandparents who can encourage such talent also cultivate the child's imagination and creativity. Children who are left uninspired by such vital gifts grow up to be uninspired adults. One grandmother plays "restaurant," with menus, waitress aprons, and play money. She realizes that she is ushering her youngsters into math, role playing, cooking, social skills, and just plain fun. They love it.

Mentor, Teacher, Wise Guy

Perhaps an invitation to explore talents and art forms makes you feel a little self-conscious. Some of us feel more like a klutz than an artist. Some of us would rather work on scenery than be actors or chanters. That's okay. Every artist and teacher feels that way at some point. It is part of the process. The only thing that drives them past that point is the burning passion to express themselves and to communicate what they are sensing and thinking. As grandparents, we too have a desire to give and an interest in our grandchildren that will help us forget ourselves and look at their needs.

There is a good description of this process in the introduction to *Story Sunday* written by John Aurelio (Paulist Press). It is a very fine collection of fairy tales composed of priestly compassion for youngsters who sit through sermons. On a monthly basis, Father would read stories that illustrated points in Scripture, until he ran out of material.

> That happened on Panic Saturday (the day before Story Sunday....) I had one of my usual confrontations with the Lord.
> "That's it! I can't find one...I've read German, Irish, Polish and even Grimm ones and I've got nothing but a headache. What do I do now?" ...
> "My grace is sufficient." ...
> I took an aspirin and sat down in my Think Chair. I tried talking to the Lord again but he wouldn't communicate.... I sulked and thought. Gradually, ever so gradually, but continuously, a story began to take shape.[15]

Each of us actually has a museum's worth of favorite pictures, stories, and songs inside our hearts; and each grandchild has a story-song-picture place inside that aches to be filled. They park themselves in front of television sets for days, hoping that something will captivate them. We can have confidence. There is a delicious blend of bonding and doing that can make all we share captivating. We become mentors, wizards, and teachers, without even trying. When we do meaningful things together, "children are absorbed in the world by emotional osmosis. . . . They find that work, play, love, and learning are fused into a single experience."[16]

Fostering growth and learning is part of our role as parent, then grandparent. Children need us to understand their world. We respond without necessarily seeing ourselves as teachers. Clifford learned to count from his great-grandpa. The old man would stand at the top of the stairs and call the tiny boy. Clifford would scurry up and wrap himself in great-grandpa's arms. Then they would walk down together, counting each of the nine steps. At the bottom they would dance a little jig.

It can be helpful to look at just how much teaching we do as a natural part of our relationships with grandchildren. We do many important things. I would like to let my left brain run wild and list three different kinds of teaching that we may find ourselves involved in:

1. mastery of human skills — like tying shoes and cooking,

2. educational ventures (also found in schools) — like memorizing the names of constellations or trees,

3. catechesis — "Efforts which help individuals and communities acquire and deepen Christian faith and identity through initiation rites, instruction, and formation of conscience."[17]

We are actually involved in all three to some extent, although parents, schools, and churches have primary responsibility. As we incorporate children into our lives, we teach them basic human skills. Table manners and telling time are good examples. The more we do ordinary things together, the more of this learning occurs. We also broaden a grandchild's view of life by teaching human skills from a different slant than their parents. We become involved in educational ventures according to our own knowledge and background. Tony teaches his grandsons three Italian words every time he visits them. Bernie shares her books with an older granddaughter. We convey religious values through experiences like burying a loved one or celebrating Easter.

We can enhance this natural learning by adding conscious efforts to teach our grandchildren. An experience like going to the zoo can be chosen as an educational opportunity. Children have a natural curiosity that can be channelled and celebrated. Mary's zoo trips include three things to make them educational ventures. The first is background preparation. It may be a conversation about when the zoo was built or how many animals it houses. It might be a stop at the library to get a book about particular animals they will search for. The second educational activity is questioning. This can be as simple as wondering out loud at something new. Children may not be interested in the answers to your musings but will soon bring up observations and questions of their own. Statements like "I wonder how tall that giraffe is?" or "What do you suppose ostriches eat?" stimulate thinking. A third educational activity is summarizing and putting different kinds of information together. In this example, a child might be encouraged to read some of the signs near animal cages. Another option would be discussing what each person liked best on the way home. Sharing feelings and judgments are appropriate. "The largest animal was.... The most intelligent animal was...."

Religion, Anyone?

Deliberate efforts to teach our grandchildren are most often weakest in the area of catechesis. Our faith seems too personal. We may also think that classrooms and pulpits are the place for religious education and nuns and priests are the better teachers. And yet *we* want to bring our grand-children to God. These opposing expectations don't make sense together. Our desires can lead to specific activities to share religion. We can make "efforts to deepen Christian faith and identity." This can be done in two ways: through activities that treat religious subject matter, or by bringing our ordinary activities into God's presence through prayer and meditation.

Once again, children learn most easily about their faith through the concretes of visual, literary, and performing arts. The artistic stance toward our world is based on reflection and imagination. Both are key ingredients in faith also. Children start with a feeling, touching stance toward reality, then move on to how God feels from the inside. Pictures, songs, and stories can be about Jesus, my First Communion, Easter, or forgiveness in our family. Some people also begin by springboarding off a "secular" drawing or activity the child has done.

When I was about nine I brought an eggshell mosaic home from school. I trudged up the back stairs to show my grand-mother. She was delighted, as usual. Memere went one step further, though, into the realms of catechesis. She brought out a picture of her friend, St. Frances Cabrini, and asked me to make another mosaic. My grandmother helped me crack more eggs and color the shells. Then I went to work. I was intrigued by the idea of being a saint. I had never thought about it before. When I finished my masterpiece, Memere presented me with a child's biography of Frances. She also hung the mosaic on a wall. When I was twenty-five, she gave it back to me as a gift. It was really only good for the trash bin at that point, but Cabrini and sainthood were already a part of my own faith, so it didn't matter.

You will find your own activities, stories, and perfor-mances that bring faith to life. Barbara looks for craft ideas and projects whenever she is in a store. Her most important criteria is that "they aren't messy." We all have our limits. If you would like a lot of suggestions, try my book *Becoming a Sensuous Catechist* in the bibliography. It is also designed to help people overcome inhibitions about the creative process. As I recall, my own children took its message to heart. After I completed the first chapter, I left it on the kitchen table to get Timothy in his crib. When I got back, Rachel and Peter had used several pages to make paper lanterns. All my hard work was hanging from the chandelier. We mustn't take ourselves too seriously. After all, God has a sense of humor. God can be a real "wise guy" sometimes.

If you want to be involved in a grandchild's religious education on more than an occasional basis, it would be wise to check with parents first. Two grandmothers I know who were concerned about their grandchildren became parish catechists. Neither would consider herself to be a teacher, but they found ways to reach out. Carol is a classroom aid for the kids her daughter teaches. She enjoys giving individual attention to the children. Monica and her husband offered to teach their grandson's class if the director would give them only six children. They just began a fourth year with "their" boys. The desire to share God's love can be a call to service. There are so many children who need grandmothers and grandfathers in faith, but won't have them unless we act.

This would be a good place to remind ourselves that we want to concretize *only* the faith that we have in common with our grandchildren. If they are Christians of another denomination, we may want to share about the person of Jesus, but not about saints or sacraments. If they are non-Christians, then we can share about "Life" and about "Happiness," leaving conclusions aside. We can answer their curiosity about our beliefs with honest, personal statements. We can also express confidence in their ability to choose a religion when they are older.

Our desire to bring grandchildren to God can spur us into action, but it must also lead us to the brink of quiet reflection together. After we enjoy learning activities, it is time to step into God's presence. Dealing with religious subject matter is only a part of the picture. Prayer, or worship, is another essential ingredient. For little ones, it is helpful to associate prayer with something tangible. This can be done by sitting in a special place with a lighted candle or closing our eyes together or using the Sign of the Cross. Children can learn meditation at a very early age because of their imaginations. For further guidelines in using prayer with children read *Our Treasured Heritage*, by Theresa Scheihing, listed in the bibliography.

There are movements of heart and mind in prayer that can be shared with children. Many stories and religious songs express both emotion and faith. Prayer can also arise from a child's experiences with strong needs or pleasures. When our son Peter was little and sick, he would call out, "Come pray with me!" Physical comfort and care can be coupled with prayer, creating a very concrete sign of God's love for a child. Some children, like some adults, are keenly aware of goodness and can learn to thank God for simple pleasures. When Beth is in a store she always notices three or four pretty dresses. Her grandmother might help her gather all three into her arms and thank God for them, and for the people who sewed them, before returning them to the rack. When I can't or shouldn't buy something I like, I do the same thing. Then I add a moment of prayer for the person who will buy my favorite item.

There are also prayers that begin with God's qualities or revelation to us. These require an actual beginning point, an effort to step into "God's space and brain," so-to-speak. We can start with a Bible story or a religious symbol and simply describe what we experience out loud. As we give voice to God's goodness, the movement of God's Spirit will bring grandchild and adult into areas of praise and meditation. Beverly likes to share night prayers with her grandchildren when visiting. She talks with each one about his or her day. Then she retells a Bible story with the child in it. Prayers arise from either of these two activities. With preschoolers, Beverly just does "thank-you prayers" for different body parts. Hugh and Doris include grandchildren in their mealtime prayers. John always prays before he starts his car. These are a few opportunities to acknowledge God, whose own acknowledgment of us sustains life. If prayer is not a regular part of your daily life, perhaps you need a revitalization of your own relationship with God. If it is, ask a grandchild to join you, from time to time, rather than rushing from one relationship to another.

Giving Ourselves Away Together

Life and growth are the fabric of family. Children get taller, smarter, and older. There is growth in numbers, from three children, to five grandchildren, to twelve and more. We experience marriages, births, deaths, and more marriages, almost according to a biological and spiritual rhythm. In my own life, I have buried close family members midway through three out of my five pregnancies. There is a building that occurs with all these comings and goings. Part of this building happens when we minister to each other, when we accept God's invitation to the soul-stretching growth that is service. Children are meant to be a part of this growth also.

Pearsall brings up the very important point that families should not be totally child-centered. One of the most effective way of guarding against such a problem is challenging young people to become involved in service. At the risk of subverting my own idea of spiritual grandparenting, I would like to quote:

> There is no such thing as "parenting." When our society made the word "parent" into a verb, it suggested that parents do something to children. In fact, there is only "familying," parents and children sharing development together and raising each other.[18]

We can train and inspire grandchildren to raise and serve each other. As grandparents, we have a broad concern for the whole family that is truly a ministry and can be a source of empowerment for others. We can be like watchdogs, alerting others to problems and needs. Inviting our families to share the gift of service is not as easy as inviting them to Thanksgiving dinner or a movie. We are asking for a commitment. A very different kind of invitation is involved, but an important one.

Josephine was worried about her granddaughter Sue, who was expecting her third child. Sue had been seriously ill during her last pregnancy and was cautioned about future dangers. Josephine called another granddaughter, Claire, and explained her concern. "I wish you could help her," she concluded. Claire sent her cousin a few maternity shirts and a book called *Praying for Your Unborn Child* by Francis and Judith MacNutt (Garden City, N.Y.: Doubleday, 1988). Sue was delighted and used both gifts throughout her pregnancy. There was much rejoicing when Sue gave birth to a healthy baby girl.

Josephine's family experienced growth through service, because many important elements were already in place. First, we must rely on the wholeness of our own relationships with individuals in the family. If these relationships are not in good repair, things will get complicated or strained. Second, we must build on habits of daily concern for others. Little children can be taught to help set the table for family gatherings. Older ones can wash dishes or load a dish washer. When they are adults, we hope they will instinctively serve others. Persons of any age who are not accustomed to helping can be invited to piggy-back another person's needs on their own doings. For example, a grown child who is going to the store for Pepsi can pick up milk too.

Grandchildren can experience service as a by-product of our lives and learn alongside us. The phenomenon of ministry often exists in concentric circles around our relationship with them. These circles build on one another: (1) actions that meet a grandparent's needs, (2) actions that meet family needs, and (3) actions that meet world needs. The first category requires honesty and humility on our part. Simple things like looking for Grandpa's glasses or reaching a can on a high shelf are acts of service. These things come naturally in some cases, but can be cultivated in most relationships with a grandchild. We do not want the impersonal, lopsided role of a gift-giver, too unreal to have daily needs. We want a give-and-take between us that can weather the years and provide a healthy model for family relationships.

The second category includes actions that meet family needs. A grandchild might bake a pie for a holiday meal, or learn to shop for a parent's birthday gift. When we see family needs, our first response should not necessarily be, "What should I do?" but "Who can help?" If it is appropriate, we can invite a grandchild to join us in service.

Angela's daughter broke her arm. It was a painful break and would be in a cast for several weeks. Angela wanted to help her daughter with laundry and housecleaning. Since her own shoulder was prone to bursitis, she asked Angela's niece to come with her and do some of the heavier chores. For three weeks, they worked together; then at the end of their commitment, they enjoyed a nice lunch out together. There are times when we cannot be involved in helping at all but can coordinate services. This is very important in family life.

The final category includes actions that meet world needs. Again, such an invitation is most effective if we are inviting a grandchild to serve along with us. Sally has often included her grandson in her weekly visits to elderly parishioners. Mark sometimes brings Brian when he cooks at a local soup kitchen. The possibilities are as endless as the different kinds of ministry and service we have chosen for ourselves. Children need opportunities to feel important and useful. It helps them discover their own inner compassion, talents, and vocation. We can offer them a kind of apprenticeship. They can try on roles of service, while receiving support from us. We can provide a model for doing a job out of kindness and faith.

It is part of grandparenting to want a meaningful relationship with a young person. This is often achieved when we choose life-giving activities, flowing from a well-balanced Christian outlook on what life is. We can work at spending regular time with individual grandchildren in order to share a fullness of life with them. We can place a high priority on learning, service, prayer, and upbuilding forms of leisure. We can invite family members to become involved with each other in building family, especially in time of need. You will find many possibilities, and activities that will become nourishing tools for the growth of elders, grandchildren, extended family, and our world community.

≺ ο ≻

For Reflection, Sharing, and Discussion

1. How do you feel about the pattern and frequency of time spent together in your family? What part do scheduling and appointments play in relationships with grandchildren?

2. How are you a teacher to your grandchildren? Are you most comfortable teaching basic human skills, being involved in purposeful educational activities, or participating in catechetical projects?

3. What role does service play in your life? How could your share your concerns and ministry with grandchildren?

Activities

1. Make a chart of your favorite leisure activities. Compare your chart with family members and grandchildren. Perhaps you can use this activity as a first step in making a date.

ACTIVITY	COST	LAST TIME	WITH WHOM	WHAT I LIKE
swimming	$2	last month	alone, or with kids	feeling weightless

2. Choose a story book for a grandchild. Make a tape of yourself reading it. Indicate when it is time to turn the page. This can be done with a bell or just by hitting a spoon on the table.

3. Write a story with a grandchild. (This is like playing chess by mail.) Begin with a few sentences, as below. Ask the young person to add another paragraph and return it for more....

   Sylvia hadn't gone into the back yard all winter. But today spring was in the air. She wandered around picking up dead branches, when behind a row of hedge she noticed....

4. Get some chalk and try sidewalk art with your youngster.

5. Decorate a shoe box, turning it into "Grandma and Grandpa's Treasure Chest." Leave a different object in it for each visit. Share sensory impressions and stories about the item. Try a religious object once, as a way to share faith.

6. Involve grandchildren in making a quilt for a new cousin. Each child can contribute an old shirt or pajamas. Cut squares. Mail an assortment of squares back to each child, so everybody can sew a few together. Assemble.

7. Make button clappers. Fold a strip of (shirt) cardboard in half. Glue buttons inside on the ends, so that they hit each other. Use them to imitate heartbeats, sounds, music. Try chanting too.

CHAPTER 7

Crisis Grandparenting

I ASKED MARION what she liked to do with her grand-children. She replied, "That's an easy question. I like to hold them, just hold them in my arms, on my lap, and in my heart." Marion's simple words express that longing we have to nurture our loved ones. She is more keenly aware of this desire as a gift from God because it has been strengthened and tested by crisis. On a physical level it is hard for Marion to hold any of her grandchildren because of chronic bursitis in both shoulders. Often she must leave that enjoyable task to her husband.

On an emotional and spiritual level, Marion has watched her extended family struggle with divorce, addictions, and serious illness. Last year, her newest granddaughter, Terry, was born with a hole in her heart. The child also developed asthma as an infant. For the first eighteen months, doctors struggled to manage both conditions at once, hoping the hole would repair itself, but it only got larger. Surgery was the only answer for Terry, even though it would be very dangerous because of her asthma. Marion ached with the desire to hold this little girl and kiss her and make everything better. It was a challenge to release Terry into the doctor's care. Marion went to Mass and placed little Terry in the Lord's hands, begging Jesus for help. She asked her daughter's permission to anoint the baby with holy oils and say an Our Father before the operation. Beth said yes, and so they prayed together. Jesus heard them. The operation was successful. The family has once again been strengthened by crisis.

In the course of our lives and families we come up

against all manner of troubles. Perhaps our holiday plans are thwarted by tragedy or divorce. Perhaps we have a broken relationship with a grown child. Maybe a family member is facing drug addiction, criminal charges, or terminal illness. For some, not sharing the same religious faith, values, or commitments translates into anxiety and crisis. These things and many others can frustrate us in our desire to nurture and love. This frustration is what we want to face in a final chapter about spiritual grandparenting. This unnerving, unholy turn of events can be a key to the power of God's Spirit among us.

Ben's youngest son, Todd, called at 9 P.M. on a Friday night. There was something awful in his voice. Ben held his breath as he groped for some terrible news in Todd's unfolding story.

Pain spilled out as the young father of three explained that he had just lost his job, a job he had relocated for only seven months earlier. Todd's boss was going bankrupt. Ben could sympathize with Todd's sense of anger and failure as a provider. The awful pain in his son's voice plunged Ben into the past, when Todd was just a small boy. He heard himself blurting out, "Todd, just get in the car and come home!" Then he stopped and realized how foolish that sounded. Todd was a man now with a family of his own.

Grandparents have hearts that have been shaped and trained by the love given to family. But that love takes on new dimensions and limits when crises emerge. As we embrace these limits, we can experience new power and strength. This is not easy when one of our "babies" is besieged by misfortune. Actually, it is impossible alone, so Marion turned to Jesus at a Mass. When we face a crisis, do we turn to the God of power and hope, who invites us to drink deeply of God's Spirit? Do we experience the gifts of God's Spirit: the peace to reclaim loved ones, the discernment to see things clearly, the courage to face needs, the gift of intercessory prayer, and the strength to become involved in crisis grandparenting? Let's look at each of these gifts and how we can receive them.

Reclaiming My Own

A crisis is by its very nature complicated. A crisis often plunges us into confusion, washing us with a flood of emotions and conflicting needs. Clarity and discernment are rare as a first response to family crisis. More often, we feel paralyzed and drawn to action at the same time. This is part of our human condition, so aptly described in Scripture. Remember the story about the apostles in a storm-tossed boat, with Jesus asleep in the stern on a cushion? They were filled with panic and awoke Jesus to deal with their crisis.

> "Master, do you not care? We are going down!" And he woke up and rebuked the wind and said to the sea, "Quiet now! Be calm!" And the wind dropped.... Then he said to them, "Why are you so frightened? How is it that you have no faith?" — Mark 4:39–40

Perhaps you have been awakened by troubled family members, expecting all kinds of help, expecting new calmness. It is only natural for them to turn to a loved one, like the apostles did. It is also normal for you to feel a tug of the heart-strings and the flow of adrenaline in response to the storm in their hearts. We want to hold them, like Marion. We want to reclaim them, like Ben. The problem is that their crisis also puts us in a precarious position, alongside them in the boat. We must realize that Jesus is in the boat too, ready to help. We must reclaim Jesus as intimately and emotionally involved, even though it seems like he is asleep. He will calm our own hearts and help us love them. Jesus did not shy away from lepers, blindness, death, or even evil spirits.

Joanne Smith describes the generous love of her grandparents:

> Two years ago my house burnt down. On the night of the fire, my grandfather sped through about three red lights, just to see if my family was all right. Then my parents couldn't find an apartment. For four months, we lived at my grandparents'

house. You're always welcome there, whether you are going to live there or just visit. My grandparents are kind, loving, and caring. Anywhere you go in the house, you'll see either a crucifix or a rosary. They are very devout Catholics.[19]

Whose Trouble Is This?

When an ambulance dispatcher answers a 911 call, he or she needs information. So do we when there is a crisis. We need to know what the problem entails and who is involved if we are to be of any help. God wants to offer peace and wisdom in our search for answers. After Jesus calmed the storm, he asked questions: "Why were they frightened?...Had they turned to the Father in prayer?" He will give us questions and discernment too. Perhaps the most important question is "Whose problem is this?" We need to recognize whose life is in crisis, in the most primary sense. Then we need to acknowledge those involved in a secondary sense, because of their family ties. We are not professionals, only grandparents. Personal relationships are an important reference point in a family crisis, with all the messiness and beauty they entail. The answer to this question must shape our response.

I would propose three categories of troubles that call for crisis grandparenting. First, there are those that affect the grandparent in a primary way, such as retirement, illness, and the death of a spouse. Second, there are crises that belong to a grown child and/or grandchild, such as remarriage, abortion, or child abuse. Third, the problems may belong to several generations because the crisis is the relationships themselves. In this last category are storm-tossed families who together need the grace of Jesus to awaken before peace will be felt.

It takes courage to examine our problems in this light. Our vision can be faulty. The boundaries of personhood and responsibility can get muddled. If we are the proud owners of a crisis, it can be overwhelming to admit it. Bill was overcome by loneliness when Sheila died. He struggled with his grief for a year, expecting grown children to fill the gap. Instead, his loneliness increased, and he began drinking a glass of wine every night at supper, which led to two, then three. He didn't like what he felt happening. A friend suggested that Bill go on a "Beginning Experience" weekend.[20] It was a good start for Bill, a chance to take responsibility for himself. His children were relieved and less pressured.

It is no less difficult to realize that our family's personal troubles are not necessarily our primary responsibility. Everett shared his experience with a grown son who telephoned when his car broke down three hundred miles from home. He asked the young man what his options were; then Everett swallowed his worries and told his son to keep in touch. He knew it was important to let him handle the emergency himself.

It is only natural that needs and emotions get enmeshed as we build families. Clarity in facing each other's needs is a life-long goal. Situations change. Children and grandchildren generate new needs and problems as life goes on. When we see them struggle with some of their problems, our own needs may be magnified or reactivated.

Janet's grandson Sean dropped out of college. He was confused about his own future and career goals, so he took a job at a gas station. Janet was reminded of her own youth. She hadn't finished high school because of her mother's illness; instead she went to work in a weaving mill. Regrets about the past were getting confused with her grandson's personal issues. Janet could not sort out Sean's primary responsibility to decide about schooling and the secondary crisis of reviewing her own life as worthwhile. It was time to give Sean the freedom to solve his own dilemma, but Janet was unable to make that decision. Instead she began to nag him, and he avoided her. Perhaps with some help, she could have faced personal regrets.

First, she might have forgiven her mother for precipitating her own crisis as a teenager. She might have taken concrete steps to respond to and fulfill her own need for intellectual stimulation. She might have enrolled in an adult education program or begun work toward an equivalency diploma. Attention to her own secondary crisis would have enabled her to be a support, a model, and a companion to her grandson as he struggled with educational goals.

Needs and Limits Are Teachable Moments

At times of crisis, family members need support to face individual needs, support without manipulation. There is a delicate balance between intimacy and independence that must be guarded. Too much closeness creates a fusion of personalities that is destructive. Too much independence creates a callous atmosphere, contrary to our faith in God. An eagle pushes its young out of the nest so it will learn to fly, but it follows as the baby bird struggles. If all goes well, it soars off in a different direction. If the eaglet fails, it swoops down only inches from the ground and brings its charge back up to the nest for another attempt. Our presence and support must first bolster the young person's own efforts, so that crisis becomes opportunity for growth and learning.

I remember swimming one day with my mother in the gentle waves off a Rhode Island beach. Since I was a new swimmer, I stopped to rest my feet on the bottom. When I did so, the water was over my head. I called to Mom in panic.

Her calm reply was, "Float for a minute, then swim back to me. I know you can do it." Her faith was reassuring. I floated long enough to trust the water again, then swam back. Had she panicked also, the story would have a different ending.

Children and grandchildren need us in time of crisis so they can "float" on our faith in them and in God. We can listen. We can tell them what we hear them saying. Most of all, we can encourage them to use personal resources in dealing with their own primary needs.

There may be times when we just don't have the objectivity to do this. There may be times when a short circuit occurs in the whole family system. To be part of such a family is to experience a large, invisible elephant roaming through the living room. The very relationships themselves seem to make matters worse. Symptoms include frequent and severe communication problems, disproportionate emotional responses to one another, and overreliance on relationships outside the family unit. Perhaps there is brokenness in two or three generations. Such a family has a great need for a Savior's love. Sometimes professional help must be sought.

What If We Flunk the Test?

This third category of family crises offers the greatest challenge to grandparents, since so many people's primary needs and responsibilities are involved; but we can take heart. There are many brothers and sisters in Jesus who have weathered such crises and have been instruments of healing and conversion for their broken families. God promises to shepherd us, even if the process takes several years. We can turn to God with misgivings about family emotional and spiritual well-being. If you are unaccustomed to following God's voice in daily life and experiencing concrete guidance, I recommend my husband John's book, *Is Talking to God a Long Distance Call?* (Ann Arbor, Mich.: Servant, 1990). I also share a friend's story with you. I'll call her Vicky.

Vicky's daughter Felicia was near the middle of her first pregnancy when she decided on a separation from her husband, Roy. Felicia came home till she could get her life reorganized, but she never had the chance. Complications arose in Felicia's pregnancy, and then after her daughter Ellen's birth new health problems emerged. When baby Ellen was less than two years old, Felicia died of cancer. Vicky's grief ushered her into daily prayer. She needed Jesus to help her with her feelings of loss as a mother and with the stamina necessary to raise a toddler. Vicky was also concerned about Roy's confusion and even hostility as he watched his in-laws raise his child.

Then, just when things were settling down, a new crisis

developed. Roy came for Ellen's fourth birthday party and told Vicky he was taking Ellen home for good. Even though everyone was upset and Ellen was frightened of him, that is exactly what Roy did. Vicky turned to her pastor for advice. He told her to pray a daily rosary for Roy's conversion. As she did, God spoke to her in two ways. First, God gave her compassion for Roy. She could have done more to foster Roy's relationship with Ellen. He must have experienced a lot of loneliness, confusion, and guilt to resort to such drastic measures. Second, Jesus gave her the courage to face her own needs and stand up for her grandchild's needs as well.

She called Roy and asked to visit Ellen. The child would need the continuity of seeing her grandparents again, to recover from these latest traumatic events. Vicky also apologized for her specific actions in the past. Roy asked for two more weeks, then three more, then another month before any visits. Vicky prayed for the strength to do the right thing. Then she turned to the Foundation for Grandparenting for support. She and her husband prayerfully decided to bring Roy to court for visitation rights but let go of any claims for custody. When the hearing came, the judge helped them all arrive at a new respect for one another. He ruled in favor of a three-hour visit every two weeks. Several years have passed since, and all of them have grown to enjoy being family together. They don't need such artificial guidelines now. Vicky's patience and the power of God's love have erased all bitterness. Even Roy's new wife has a deep affection for Vicky. She recently presented Vicky with her newborn son, saying, "I bet you never thought you would have a grandson. Well, here he is!"

Interceding Is Not Doing Nothing

We began this chapter with Marion's desire to hold her little grandchild with a heart defect. The baby's crisis also challenged her as a recovering alcoholic. She needed the support of an Alcoholics Anonymous group, her parish RENEW group, as well as her faith in Jesus, to face this crisis. It is one of God's most precious gifts that we can support one another. One way we can do this as Christians is through intercessory prayer, prayer that lifts other people from our arms into God's arms.

My favorite image for intercessory prayer is in a story about Moses (Exod. 17:8–17). He was positioned on a hill praying for his "children," the Israelites, as they fought a battle. When he lifted his outstretched arms and heart toward heaven, they would have the advantage. When he tired, and dropped his arms, they began to lose the battle. As the story goes, Aaron and Hur supported Moses' arms until sunset, when the Israelites were finally victorious.

No matter whose crisis we are facing in our families, we may need the support of others. We will surely need the support and power of a loving God. Lifting ourselves and our loved ones into God's presence is a powerful act of concern. If the crisis is our own, we must bring our needs before our creator and redeemer. If we do not, we run the risk of expecting family members to be gods in our lives, or we could possibly come to think of our loved ones as devils, keeping us from eternal happiness. If the crisis affects a grown child or grandchild's life in a primary way, intercessory prayer should be our first step, our refueling for new commitments that may lie ahead.

To intercede literally means to place oneself between. Intercessory prayer will be most fruitful if we remain flexible, as we stand between God and a loved one's problems. We must be watching in two directions at once in order to experience this kind of prayer as ministry and source of spiritual growth. Somehow, we must combine God's view of the situation, our loved one's view of it, and the actual needs. Let me give you some examples.

There are many believers who have looked at family members with God's eyes and prayed from that perspective. St. Monica prayed for her son Augustine, clinging to a vision of his goodness and call. We can be fairly certain that Anna and Joachim, the grandparents of Jesus, prayed for him as a special child of Yahweh. I know a man named Joe in a poor inner-city parish who cherishes the task of being a godfather to babies without friend or family. He is proud of a scrapbook with photographs of all fifty-four of them. They are God's children as far as Joe is concerned. He sees with faith.

There is a curious little episode in Luke's Gospel (2:22–38) that teases us into thinking that Jesus had "spiritual grandparents," not physically related to him. They were Anna and Simeon, elders given to many hours of daily prayer in the temple. Perhaps one of their greatest pleasures was holding little babies and interceding for them. When Joseph and Mary came along with baby Jesus, they took a liking to him. After all, he was probably a cute baby, not counting the usual diaper rash. As they prayed, God spoke to them through prophecies, and they shared God's viewpoint with Mary and Joseph.

Another Scripture story shows us a grandfather who was very stubborn about God's vision of his family. In Genesis 48, the old patriarch Jacob receives his son Joseph and two grandsons, Manasseh and Ephraim. Family festivities and conversation culminate in a time of prayer and blessing for the two boys. Joseph positioned the older son, Manasseh, on his grandfather's right side for the preferred blessing. (This is because in those days the right hand was for eating and the left for personal hygiene.) Jacob reversed his hands, aware of the younger son's calling and leadership in God's sight, disregarding his son's protests.

We must also intercede with an eye toward the views and needs of a loved one so that we are based in reality and can let go of these needs as nurturers. We might name the feelings a loved one is experiencing or tell God what he or she feels they need. Grandparents can take all they have heard and retell it in God's ear. We can imagine how *we* might feel in their place, and thus pray with compassion. No matter how foolish or impossible, God cares about every detail in a crisis.

Finally, we may need to ask others with more objectivity

to pray with us for our families. Moses needed Aaron and Hur to help. The Body of Jesus is there for us. As we listen for God's wisdom together, we may learn about ways *we* can change, forgive, or repent that will improve the situation. If we pray alone, we are not as likely to hear such things. Jesus put himself between the Father and all of humanity, willing to do whatever it cost to intercede. It cost him everything. It will not cost us less.

Families in Crisis

After we have discerned the nature of a family crisis and brought our loved ones before God in prayer, it is time to embrace crisis grandparenting. We face new commitments. Somehow our troubled loved ones have moved ever more closely into the center of our hearts. The love that we want to give must become concrete. How that love is expressed and acted out will vary quite a bit. We must explore very personal possibilities in response to very particular circumstances. Sometimes the desire to care for them may be confused with other emotions and needs. In such cases, helping and commitment can present a paradox. It may be important to concentrate on what we *don't* say and do, out of love for those in crisis. Greg made a decision not to write or call his grandson in a treatment facility for drug abuse. He is following the advice of the professional staff at the facility, but it is hard. Greg will make a new decision later. Sometimes you may not be able to *do* anything, except admit your own helplessness; but even this feeble gift can sometimes free a loved one to admit that he or she is helpless and must search for answers in a more aggressive fashion.

Grandparents can offer the stabilizing love that so many young people need when they and their immediate families are too close to the crisis to be supportive of each other. Our commitments to them can be temporary or permanent. We may even become surrogate parents, alongside or in place of our grown children. Again, we must look for very personal ways of being available, while not violating the primary responsibilities of other family members. Our commitment can be as simple as a daily rosary and a weekly phone call or as complicated as seeking legal custody. Our hearts and common sense and faith will lead the way. Let me share some stories to illustrate levels of commitment.

Nora's daughter was having problems handling several of her teenagers after her husband's sudden death. The oldest girl had already left home under unpleasant circumstances. Penny was threatening to do the same thing. Nora offered her home to Penny for the summer. She set down rules and responsibilities for Penny and also lavished her with attention when she wanted it. The young girl settled down and was able to return home.

Sid and Dolores had a grandson, Peter, who broke his hip in a car accident. They visited him every day in the hospital. This was a big help, because both Peter's parents worked full time and had four other young children. When Peter was released from the hospital, Sid and Dolores took turns doing his physical therapy with him. Sid took photographs of the boy's progress. When he was finally able to walk without help or special equipment, they had a little party at their house.

Josephine's pregnant daughter, Pam, married a boy named Larry. Just a few months after little Bonny's birth, the young man died in a car accident. Josephine welcomed Pam and the new baby into her home; but even then, Pam couldn't adjust to being a teenage widow and parent. She turned to drug abuse and eventually ran away with a pimp to nearby Chicago. By the time Bonny was five, Pam had abandoned her, except for a few stressful visits. After one such visit, Josephine and little Bonny were watching a television special about Carol Burnett. They huddled on the maroon flowered sofa together, trying to make sense out of the tangled relationships in their lives. Just then, an interviewer asked Carol Burnett how she felt about being neglected by her mother and raised by her grandmother. Carol's answer touched the desolate pair. They remember her as saying, "It doesn't matter what my mother did. What matters is being taken care of by somebody who really loves you, like my grandmother did." Josephine and Bonny gave each other's hand a little squeeze. It was just a formality for the courts to grant custody of Bonny to Josephine a few months later.

In all of these examples, there were a lot of negotiations between grandparent and grown child about the welfare of grandchildren. Some of the negotiations were productive. Some were not. All of the conversations were emotionally challenging. When grandparents find themselves offering housing or sharing parental responsibilities, even more negotiations are needed. It can be helpful to realize a distinction between reclaiming family by letting them move in and setting up a new lifestyle for all persons concerned. These are two separate realities.

If They Move In, Does God Move Out?

Tom and Alice came for counseling with a lot of unresolved anger and guilt. Three divorced daughters had moved back into their home with four children among them. Tom and Alice had no privacy, no additional income for extra food, no agreements about household responsibilities; even their bedroom was pressed into service as a place to change diapers. These grandparents made several attempts to discuss their own needs but failed. Their question was, "How can we possibly stop being *nice* to our own children?" They couldn't. The only solution was for them to sell their home and move into a one-bedroom apartment.

When we offer our homes, and grandparenting, in tandem with our grown children, we are accepting a commitment as drastic as the day we married many years ago. New agreements must be negotiated. Even though our young people look the same, they are not. They have been changed by (a) graduating or quitting school, (b) getting married or divorced, or (c) getting pregnant and giving birth. No suitcases should be unpacked, no babies driven home from a hospital, no furniture moved, until all the parties involved negotiate a new way of life. I will not be living in your house, so it makes no difference what guidelines I would suggest. You must come up with your own specific rules and review them together at specific intervals.

If you don't know what I mean, I list some possibilities on page 135. Show this page to your grown children. Choose some rules together. Paste them on the refrigerator door and throw yourselves on the mercy of God. If suitcases have already been unpacked, take yourself by the hand and admit that you made a mistake; then show them this page. There will be fallout; but the damage done to your grandchildren may be irrevocable if you don't. We are not raising homing pigeons. We want to empower our families to face reality.

Such agreements may not have been necessary two or three generations back, when many of our immigrant ancestors considered it a privilege to care for one another. We are living in different times. We have a false security in our own independence and unrealistic expectations of the nuclear family. Even though the healing love and affirmation of the extended family is becoming more important, we don't remember how it works. We, as grandparents, are revolutionaries in realizing this ministry as it flows from a God-given desire to nurture our own. Let us turn to our God and find ways to embrace crisis grandparenting. God's right arm will uphold us and make us strong together.

> Nothing therefore can come between us and the love of Christ, even if we are troubled or worried.... For I am certain of this: neither death nor life, no angel, no prince, nothing that exists, nothing still to come, not any power, or height or depth, nor any created thing, can ever come between us and the love of god made visible in Christ Jesus our Lord.
>
> — Romans 8:35, 38–39

1. We will ask of each other only what we need, understanding that a response will be forthcoming. By expressing only needs that are important to us, we will free our family members from an undue sense of obligation.[21]

2. We value time spent in common and will eat at least six meals together weekly.

3. The owners of the home have final say in how it is used and how space is allotted.

4. Parents will help children take responsibility for their actions. Grandparents will do so only in the absence of parents.

5. All adults will share financial responsibility for the care and upkeep of the household.

6. All persons over the age of seven will have assigned tasks in service for the family.

7. We will work to affirm each others' marriages.

8. This agreement will be reviewed weekly (Saturday, 7 P.M). When a conflict cannot be resolved, we will call _____ (Fr. Paul, Uncle Ned, etc.) to meet with us. If we cannot find a solution within seven days, we will go back to the living arrangement prior to this agreement.

9. We hope to rely on the power of God's healing love to help us.

For Reflection, Sharing, and Discussion

1. What part does suffering play in your life? Which is harder to experience, a crisis in your life or in a loved one's life? Why?

2. Make a list of all your fears, large and small. Then put them in order with the worst one at the top of the list. What kind of crises do these fears point toward? Would each one be your crisis, a loved one's, or a crisis in the whole family system? Perhaps you would like to compare your list with a spouse or family member's list.

3. What is your experience with intercessory prayer? How could you benefit from this kind of prayer?

4. What are your fondest dreams for your grandchildren? How might you help them realize these dreams? What commitments have you made to your grandchildren?

Resources

For information about intergenerational education:
Dr. Sally Newman, Generations Together, 600A Thackery Hall, University of Pittsburgh, Pittsburgh, PA 15260

For help with grandparents' visitation rights:
Grandparents'–Children's Rights, Inc. 5728 Bayonne Ave. Haslett, MI 48840

For general information:
Foundation for Grandparenting, Box 31, Lake Placid, NY 12946. This organization helps "assure grandparents their rightful place in society" through education, research, and support of projects and individuals. Major areas of interest and activity for the foundation include:

1. Work toward uniform grandparents' visitation rights.

2. The "Centrum Project": a multigenerational elementary school. "Elders start school with the youngsters and get

promoted with them until the sixth grade." Each child has a "grandparent."

3. Grandparent Network: a central clearing house for information about intergenerational projects such as Grandparents' Day in schools and Expectant Grandparent programs in hospitals.

4. A grandparent newsletter called the *Vital Connection*. For subscriptions write Box 954, Burlington, VT 05402.

Conclusion

Any genealogy chart will show you what it takes to be a physical grandparent, just two successive acts of procreation that result in live births. I think most of us want to add more to the story than that. We want to share life with children and grandchildren in some meaningful way, thus becoming spiritual grandparents. When we choose the unimaginable love of Father, Son, and Spirit as the wellspring of relationships between the generations, then even deeper depths and wider widths are possible. We are empowered as companions to our grandchildren in the richest sense. We can build bridges and stronger families alongside our grown children.

There are many styles of spiritual grandparenting that encompass decisions and activities involving our most human selves. We can offer "feeling places" for the celebration of holidays. We can offer a family history that anchors individuals, especially through storytelling. We can watch for natural paths to a lively faith in God. We can choose life-giving activities that call grandchildren to grow in unique talents. We can stand beside them when crisis challenges every fiber of our loved ones' souls.

Perhaps many of these things have already been happening in your life. If so, praise God! More is also possible. It is time to choose one more small step. God will help us decide what comes next. If we have no relationship with our grandchildren, then a more serious and ongoing effort is called for. We must face our new desires and the results of the past at the same time. It may mean repentance on our part and bruised expectations all around. But it is important to try.

Some grandparents have such a strong desire to nurture that they go beyond physical ties to choose grandchildren. I have introduced you to a few of them. Karen and Richard are such people. They supported a Grandparent's Day at a local elementary school and recruited friends to be honorary grandparents for children who needed some. Their own Melissa shared a poem about them during the day. That's how Karen found out that she has "young hair" and Richard discovered that he is "not very wealthy." Perhaps you are called to be this kind of a grandparent as well, no matter what kind of hair you have.

We began this book with a trip to Notre Dame Church in Worcester. I would like to end with a pilgrimage to Notre Dame Church in Quebec City. John and I celebrated our twentieth anniversary with a journey to common ancestral soil. It was a joyous second honeymoon and a much-needed respite from the task of parenting five children. We experienced the rare privilege of worshipping in the three-hundred-year-old cathedral where more than fifty of our ancestors' marriages took place. Grandparents from families named Langlois, Boucher, Miville, Huode, Hebert, LeTardif, Gosselin, and Cote had prayed at the same gold altar, under the same roof with the paintings of a vast blue sky. There have been renovations and rebuildings since those marriages in the 1600s, but the same vital faith in a holy God has been passed down to us. God's faithfulness to our family has lasted over three hundred years.

Now John and I must respond, "Amen!" and somehow fulfill many grandparents' deepest longings in doing so. Faith is a gift that each individual and household must choose for themselves, like Joshua did. Then that choice stands as a beacon and an invitation to the next generation.

> Choose today whom you wish to serve.... As for me and my House, we will serve Yahweh.
> — Joshua 24:14–15

The trip to Quebec helped me rejoice in God's lavish gift of faith to families. God has made promises to us that are stronger than death and time. We can rejoice in what

God wants to do for our children, grandchildren, and great-grandchildren. I believe God loves them. I believe God forgives them. I believe they are called to eternal and outrageous happiness in God's presence. What do you believe? As I sat in that old cathedral the words of a song and prophecy welled up inside my heart, echoing down the centuries. It was the same song that consoled me when Mom died fifteen years ago this summer. I share it with you now.

> Do not be afraid, for I have redeemed you;
> I have called you by name, you are mine.
> Should you pass through the sea, I will be with you;
> or through rivers, they will not swallow you up.
> For I am . . . your God . . . your savior.
>
> I will bring your offspring from the east,
> and gather them from the west, . . .
> all those who bear my name,
> whom I have created for my glory. . . .
>
> For I will pour out water on the thirsty soil,
> streams on the dry ground.
> I will pour my spirit on your descendants,
> my blessings on your children.
>
> (Do not be afraid, for I have redeemed you;
> I have called you by your name, you are mine.)
>
> — Isaiah 43:2–3, 5–7 and 44:3–4

Notes

1. Andrew J. Cherlin and Frank Furstenberg, Jr., *The New American Grandparent* (New York: Basic Books, 1986), 50.

2. Arthur Kornhaber, M. D., and Kenneth Woodward, *Grandparents/Grandchildren: The Vital Connection* (New York: Anchor Press/Doubleday, 1981), introduction.

3. Antoine de Saint-Exupéry, *The Little Prince*, trans. Katherine Woods (New York, London: Harcourt Brace Jovanovich, 1971), 57.

4. Gertrud Mueller Nelson, *To Dance with God: Family Ritual and Community Celebration* (New York/Mahwah, N.J.: Paulist Press, 1986), 41.

5. Ibid., 25.

6. Charles J. Keating, *Dealing with Difficult People* (New York/Ramsey, N.J.: Paulist Press, 1984), 81.

7. Dolores Curran. "It's Not Your Fault If Your Kids Leave the Church," *U.S. Catholic* (September 1988).

8. Ethel Barrett, *Storytelling: It's Easy* (Grand Rapids, Mich.: Zondervan Publishing House, 1960), 11.

9. Gabriele Lusser Rico, *Writing the Natural Way* (Los Angeles: J. P. Tarcher, 1983), 51.

10. *Catholic Evangelization Today*, Kenneth Boyack, C.S.P., ed. (New York/Mahwah, N.J.: Paulist Press, 1987).

11. *Sharing the Light of Faith, National Directory for Catholics of the United States*, United States Catholic Conference, Department of Education, 1979, 22.

12. Donald B. Conroy and Charles J. Fahey, "Christian Perspective on the Role of Grandparents," in *Grandparenthood*, Vern L. Bengtson and John F. Robertson, eds. (Beverly Hills, Calif.: Sage Publications, 1985), 197.

13. Bert Ghezzi, *Keeping Your Kids Catholic* (Ann Arbor, Mich.: Servant Publications, 1989), 22–24.

14. *Catholic Evangelization Today*, 113.

15. John Aurelio, *Story Sunday* (New York/Ramsey, N.J.: Paulist Press, 1978), foreword.

16. Arthur Kornhaber, M. D., and Kenneth Woodward, *Grandparents/Grandchildren: The Vital Connection*, 172.

17. *National Catechetical Directory*, 3.

18. Paul Pearsall, Ph.D., *The Power of the Family* (New York: Doubleday, 1990), 28.

19. Joanne Smith, Michael Hayes, Amy Unetich, Jason Amplo, and Christopher Lambot represent fifty children at St. Ignatius School in Hicksville, N.Y., who participated in a writing project to explore feelings about grandparents. My thanks to the principal, Jacqueline Burdi, and the staff.

20. The Beginning Experience is a weekend enrichment program for people who are widowed, separated, or divorced for at least a year. Sharings and activities help individuals adjust to a new life. Contact your diocesan office of family life or write Beginning Experience Central Office, 305 Michigan Ave., Detroit, MI 48226.

21. Paul Pearsall, "Twelve Articles of Family Faith," in *The Power of the Family*, 284.

Bibliography

Barber, Lucie W. *The Religious Education of Preschool Children.* Birmingham, Ala.: Religious Education Press, 1981.

Barrett, Ethel. *Storytelling: It's Easy.* Grand Rapids, Mich.: Zondervan Publishing House, 1960.

Beller, Susan Provost. *Roots for Kids.* White Hall, Va.: Betterway Publishing, 1989.

Bengtson, Vern L., and John F. Robertson, eds. *Grandparenthood.* Beverly Hills, Calif.: Sage Publications, 1985.

Boucher, Therese. *Becoming a Sensuous Catechist: Using the Arts in Religious Education.* Mystic, Conn.: Twenty-Third Publications, 1984.

Bloomfield, Harold H., and Leonard Felder. *Making Peace with Your Parents.* New York: Ballantine Books, 1983.

Boyack, Kenneth, C.S.P., ed. *Catholic Evangelization Today.* New York/Mahwah, N.J.: Paulist Press, 1987.

Cherlin, Andrew J., and Frank Furstenberg, Jr. *The New American Grandparent.* New York: Basic Books, 1986.

Dodson, Dr. Fitzhugh, with Paula Reuben. *How to Grandparent.* New York: Harper & Row, Publishers, 1981.

Ensley, Eddie. *Prayer That Heals Our Emotions.* Columbus, Ga.: Contemplative Books, 1986.

Faucett, Robert J., and Carol Ann Faucett. *Intimacy and Midlife.* New York: Crossroad, 1990.

Fischer, Kathleen R. *The Inner Rainbow.* New York/Ramsey, N.J.: Paulist Press, 1983.

Ghezzi, Bert, ed. *Keeping Your Kids Catholic.* Ann Arbor, Mich.: Servant Publications, 1989.

Groeschel, Benedict, Capuchin. *Stumbling Blocks and Stepping Stones: Spiritual Answers to Psychological Questions.* New York/Mahwah, N.J.: Paulist Press, 1987.

Hilton, Suzanne. *Who Do You Think You Are?* Philadelphia: Westminster Press, 1978.

Keating, Charles J. *Dealing with Difficult People.* New York/Ramsey, N.J.: Paulist Press, 1984.

Kelsey, Morton T. *Caring.* New York/Ramsey, N.J.: Paulist Press, 1981.

Kornhaber, Arthur, M. D. *Between Parents and Grandparents.* New York: St. Martin's Press, 1986.

Kornhaber, Arthur, M. D., and Kenneth Woodward. *Grandparents/ Grandchildren: The Vital Connection.* New York: Anchor Press/ Doubleday, 1981.

Linn, Dennis, S.J., and Matthew Linn, S.J. *Healing Life's Hurts.* New York/Ramsey, N.J.: Paulist Press, 1978.

Nelson, Gertrud Mueller. *To Dance with God: Family Ritual and Community Celebrations.* New York/Mahwah, N.J.: Paulist Press, 1986.

Nouwen, Henri J. M., and Walter J. Gaffney. *Aging: The Fulfillment of Life.* New York: Doubleday, 1976.

Pearsall, Paul, Ph.D. *The Power of the Family.* New York: Doubleday, 1990.

Scheihing, Theresa O'Callaghan, with Louis M. Savary. *Our Treasured Heritage: Teaching Christian Meditation to Children.* New York: Crossroad, 1981.